100

Ways to Happy Children

A Guide for Busy Parents

DR. TIMOTHY J. SHARP

MJF BOOKS
New York

Published by MJF Books
Fine Communications
322 Eighth Avenue
New York, NY 10001

100 Ways to Happy Children
LC Control Number: 2014941168
ISBN 978-1-60671-270-2

Copyright © 2009 by Timothy J. Sharp

Jacket and interior design by Danie Pout © Penguin Group (Australia)
Additional design by Evi O. © Penguin Group (Australia)

First published by Penguin Group (Australia), 2009.

This edition is published by MJF Books in arrangement
with the Penguin Group (Australia).

Printed in the United States of America.

MJF Books and the MJF colophon are trademarks of Fine Creative Media, Inc.

QF   10   9   8   7   6   5   4   3   2   1

This book is dedicated to my lovely and loving family: to my wonderful wife Marnie and to my inspirational children Tali and Coby. This book comes from them and is written for them. They constantly motivate me to seek happiness and I'm driven daily to do what I can to enhance their happiness.

Contents

Introduction

Let me ask you a simple yet important question: would you rather your child live a life without problems or a great life? This book is about actively and passionately pursuing happiness for your children as opposed to simply minimising their problems. It is about helping your child, and you, live a great life.

As well as being a father of two, I am a positive psychologist. Most of this book is based on the principles of positive psychology, often called 'the science of happiness'.

For most of its history, psychology has been concerned with what's wrong with people; its focus has been to identify and treat psychological trauma and manage serious behavioural difficulties. Positive psychology has emerged in the last couple of decades as a way of maximising the parts of ourselves that work well, increasing our levels of optimism and identifying and utilising our strengths in order to thrive.

When applied to parenting, positive psychology suggests we work with our kids to build on innate strengths and help them frame their world in a more optimistic way. It aims to establish a solid psychological base at the outset, rather than wait until some serious problem or issue emerges. Positive psychology is the fence we erect at the top of the cliff to stop our children from falling, rather than the ambulance we send to the bottom of the cliff to pick up the pieces.

So how, as parents, do we build this 'fence' for our kids? To start with, we need to become good role models. The most basic truth of the dynamics of family life is that children learn how to be in this world by watching their parents. If a child's parents are fearful and negative the child will learn that the world is a difficult and dangerous place; if the parents are positive, healthy and happy the child will learn that life is something to be enjoyed and appreciated. Section One of this book provides specific information on how you can work to realign your priorities, better manage your key relationships, improve your levels of optimism and build on your strengths, all with the aim of creating a strong foundation for a happy family life and happy children.

The other four sections focus on aspects of your child's life and experiences, and provide specific strategies on how you can help your child reframe their outlook and reinforce the things that work well for them. Section Two, which deals with character, looks at managing negative thoughts, identifying strengths, developing decency, building resilience and setting goals. Section Three is about positive discipline and setting boundaries. Section Four focuses on how you can work with your child to make their learning years as positive and productive as possible. Section Five explores how good physical health fuels strong emotional growth and wellbeing.

This book was written specifically with busy parents in mind – which, these days, is most of us. My last book *100 Ways to Happiness: a guide for busy people* received much positive feedback regarding its format – one hundred short practical chapters that could be easily digested in minutes and did not require reading masses of psychological theory and a lot of time-consuming 'homework' for the reader. This book is written in the same style. It invites you to dip in and out as time permits, although, of course, you can read it cover to cover. Most of the chapters have a short exercise or goal, which will allow you to put your reading into practice. These exercises might be as simple as:

- remembering to give your child praise for a specific achievement
- sharing a meal around the table on a regular basis

- talking your child through a negative experience
- reading an affirming story
- setting aside time for just 'hanging out'
- setting a regular time for going to bed.

Practising a range of activities helps you help your kids build a 'portfolio' of positive experiences, which in turn helps lead them away from self-limiting beliefs or a negative mindset. This gentle step-by-step approach is often enough to recalibrate the family dynamic and create a happier home environment. Obviously, where there are more entrenched problems parents should seek further help – the Recommended Resources section on page 164 offers a list of useful contacts and further reading.

Something all parents know is that no two children are exactly the same. They are not blank slates but individuals with distinct personalities, likes and dislikes, and a seemingly fixed way of looking at the world. Some children are just born happier and more optimistic than others. Some are happy occasionally and stormy at other times. It's important to point out that positive psychology does not suggest people should be happy all the time. Rather, it recognises that humans are social and emotional beings and that it is perfectly normal for them to experience the full gamut of emotions. Negative emotions, such as distress, anger and frustration, and positive emotions, such as happiness, joy and excitement, are all part of our children's (and our) everyday lives.

While we know from research and experience that some people are just naturally happier and more optimistic than others, we also know that *optimism is something that can be learned.* Teaching a child to become an optimistic thinker is not about moulding them into some ideal of perfection. It is not social engineering or an invitation to children to avoid the difficult realities of the world we live in. Thinking optimistically is not the same thing as simply seeing the world in a positive light. It is about being able to get a realistic picture of the world in which we live – flaws and all – and then being prepared to live in that world with hope, courage and commitment. When we are optimistic we are motivated to take on the kinds of difficult challenges that help us learn and grow; we feel inspired to work with our strengths, utilise our skills, and employ our critical capacities to their fullest. We feel more inclined to help others and to connect more deeply with those we love.

100 Ways to Happy Children: a guide for busy parents is not just something I dreamt up one night – it's full of suggestions and strategies based on solid scientific research. With this in mind I can confidently state that the 'happiness program' outlined in the following pages does and will work. I'm confident in this because of the results of countless research studies from around the world, the evidence of thousands of my clients and, most importantly, because I've seen it work with my own family and my own happy children. So read on and find happiness for your kids and for yourself in these one hundred ways.

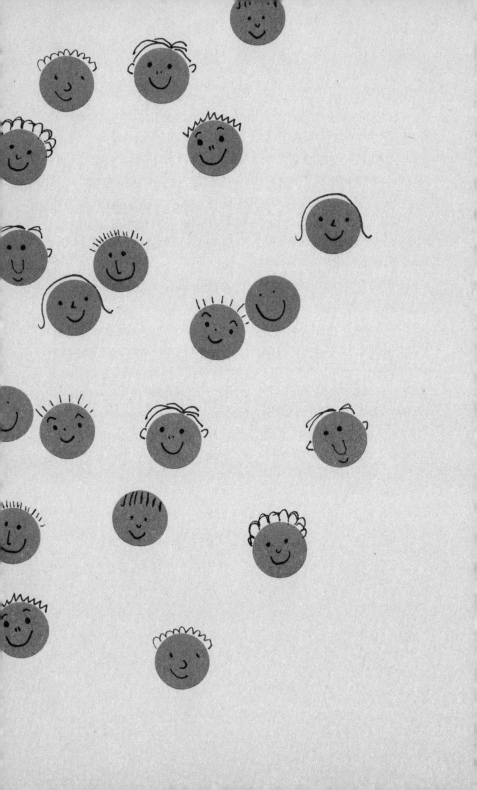

Section One

20 ways to establish family foundations

This section is more about you than it is your children, but as any parent instinctively knows their own mood has a profound affect on the mood of their children, from tiny tots to teenagers. The following twenty short chapters provide a whirlwind tour of the principles of positive psychology and give you tried-and-trusted methods for working to increase your own happiness levels. Many of the examples given relate to parenting, but some exercises ask that you take pause from this most important job and refocus on you as an individual. Happiness levels are at least partly determined by genes – yes, happiness is a heritable trait. But no child is or learns to be happy in a vacuum – they look to Mum and Dad for example and inspiration. Happy parents make happy children.

1. Happiness is . . .

What makes someone happy? What makes a happy adult and what makes a happy child? The answers to these questions are complex and varied and differ from person to person, family to family, but generally I believe that the following list contains the most significant qualities that contribute to happiness:

- having a clear sense of meaning and purpose in your life
- being active and healthy
- having meaningful relationships
- knowing and fully utilising your strengths
- living in the present moment rather than dwelling on the past or worrying about the future
- appreciating what you have rather than focusing on what you don't have and what you think you need.

Happiness is something we choose. Every day we make decisions – everything from what we're going to eat to how we're going to respond to a particular situation – and it's the nature and the quality of these decisions that determine our happiness. There's nothing mystical or magical about happiness; it's something that we create through our daily approach to the world.

When I say happiness is something we *choose*, I've selected that word carefully, because each letter relates to six key strategies that lead to happiness. You'll need **c**larity of your life goals and sense of purpose; you'll need good **h**ealth; you'll need **o**ptimism and a positive and realistic view of yourself, your future and the world; you'll need to be aware of **o**thers and your relationships; you'll need to focus on your **strengths**; and last but not least, you have to **e**njoy the moment.

This self-determining and future-focused approach is one of the most exciting aspects of positive psychology. Although steeped in scientific evidence-based theory and practice, this approach essentially says, 'Okay, we all have faults and can improve in certain areas, but we also have inherent strengths and qualities, and the more we use these, the better, happier and more successful we'll be.'

Happy people – both adults and children – are better than depressed or unhappy people at identifying and utilising their strengths, and they worry less about their weaknesses. They don't ignore their faults but they manage them so they don't interfere with success and happiness. They recover quickly from difficult circumstances and make the most of, and use, what they're really good at.

2. Happiness is not . . .

There are many myths and misunderstandings about happiness, which often lead people to look for happiness in the wrong places. I believe the problem starts because of the inappropriate definitions and expectations many people have of happiness.

A vitally important message to convey to your child is that happiness is much more than living the pleasant life and enjoying short-term highs. Instant gratification and rampant consumerism are not necessarily conducive to long and lasting positive emotions. Happiness is not directly related to:

- intelligence
- physical appearance
- wealth or income level (as long as you're not suffering extreme financial hardship)
- the number or type of toys or objects you own.

Psychologist Leaf Van Boven polled people from all walks of life about past activities and purchases, and he found that people are generally happier when they spend money on life experiences instead of material possessions. People's moods became more elevated when they recalled experiences rather than objects, even if the experience didn't seem great at the time. So to some extent, memories get rosier with hindsight but objects depreciate.

Ask yourself:

- What 'stuff' do we have that we could use to have more and better experiences?
- Do we make full use of our car to explore new places?
- Do we use our bicycles enough?
- Are there better ways to play with toys that will offer more enjoyment?

3. Actions speak louder than words

Children learn by observing – they watch you and then they copy you – so we must be the people we wish to see our children become. This is called 'modelling'.

Modelling is one of the most powerful ways of learning, and as parents we are our kids' key role models. Obviously there are others, such as teachers and grandparents, but learning begins at home. Quite simply, by being happy ourselves we model happy behaviours for our children.

The good news is that we can use this to our advantage. If your child sees you going for a walk every day they'll consider it a natural thing to do; if they see you eating fruit and vegetables instead of chocolates and chips they'll see that as normal; and if they see you smiling and laughing that will be a regular part of life for them too.

Forget the saying, 'Do as I say not as I do' – it's a waste of time. Actions speak louder than words. Your child will copy what you do far more often than they'll do what you say. Many of you will already know this from experience!

Gillian is raising her thirteen-year-old son on her own. He is bright, happy, well adjusted, sociable, plays a lot of sport, has a wide circle of friends and focuses on enjoying life. Gillian has always believed in rewards instead of punishment and she encourages her son to think for himself and negotiate the boundaries she sets for his life. Gillian recommended study when her son was a baby and she's about to complete her Master of Clinical Psychology. Her son is excited and proud of her and sees how dedication and persistence earn rewards.

4. Discuss and define family values

Your values highlight the things that matter most to you and help you determine the way you want to live your life, now and in the future. They shape your beliefs about what is right or wrong, what is important and unimportant, and what you want to focus on and what you should ignore. These values influence and drive your life goals, so they're crucial in motivating you to do what you need to do to live a successful and happy life.

For some people, the answers to these questions of values will be guided by religious and/or cultural beliefs; for others, there are more secular versions. Either way, the aim is to determine what your family stands for and, therefore, what it will reward and reinforce.

To get you started, consider this list of suggestions that many families would feel are important:

- family and relationships
- caring and sharing
- health and happiness
- diligence and perseverance
- creativity and innovation
- learning and education
- politics and the environment
- the pursuit of excellence
- spirituality and faith.

Set aside some time, with all the family present, to review this list and to add to or modify it as you see fit. Allow everyone to contribute, and use appropriate language (words that mean something to you and your child). Remember, children are never too young to learn right from wrong, so you might as well ensure that what they're learning is what you want them to learn.

5. Define your parenting style

All parents need to define their parenting style for themselves. Some reading this will be in a sole-parenting situation. For those who are co-parenting, it is important to find ways of parenting that work for both partners. Not everyone has to agree on everything, but it's confusing for children when their parents consistently disagree on everything – and this does happen.

This book offers many tools to help you define your parenting style; I hope your partner is reading it too, so you can compare observations and conclusions. Make sure you pay attention to your own personal strengths, as well as those of your partner. Your aim should be to work out with your partner how each of you can parent using individual strengths without undermining one another in the process; you are looking to complement each other not compete.

Ask yourself (and each other) the following questions:

- What behaviours do you consider appropriate or inappropriate?
- What methods of discipline do you think are reasonable?
- How do you like to use rewards and positive encouragement?
- How do you deal with stress?
- Is there a fair distribution of duties or chores around the house?

Emma's parenting style is very different from her husband's. She tends to worry about rules, discipline and doing things properly. Her husband Tony wants the kids to be able to relax and enjoy themselves. A good example of their parenting styles clashing is their different attitudes to homework. Emma has always thought their children (aged ten and twelve) should start their homework as soon as they get home. But Tony has argued that it's okay to let them sit around and watch television for an hour or so, which has really annoyed Emma because she doesn't like the television being on during the school week. Emma and Tony realised their arguments about this were confusing the kids, so they came up with a formula that works. The kids get an hour of free time after school before starting homework. They tend to read, ring their friends or do a bit of regulated Internet surfing. They don't have the television on during the week but they have a fairly free rein on the weekend.

6. What's your life plan?

This is important because your life plan will affect how you parent and how your children regard their own future.

Have you read *Alice's Adventures in Wonderland*? Like a lot of great stories it includes several very sound messages, one of which stems from a scene in which Alice asks the Cheshire Cat, 'Would you tell me, please, which way I ought to walk from here?' His response is, 'That depends a good deal on where you want to get to.'

Without a life plan you can wander aimlessly, subject to life's ebbs and flows. You may stumble upon happiness sometimes, but you won't experience nearly as much of it as you could if you were clear and focused. If you don't determine your own life plan, the chances are you'll fall into someone else's plan.

Happy people tend to have a clear sense of life purpose, which allows for greater clarity of their life direction, and of specific and measurable life goals. These people feel focused and in control – of themselves, their lives and their world.

The more specifically you set your goals and determine your life direction, the more successful and happy you will be. Happy people know what life's about; they know what sort of person they want to be, what they want to achieve and what legacy they want to leave.

Try the following exercise. Imagine you are writing and producing your own life movie; you have complete freedom to make of it what you will. While you are imagining your story take shape, focus on happiness in all aspects of your life, including your family relationships. Imagine viewing one of the scenes that takes place in about twelve months' time: life isn't necessarily 100 per cent perfect, but despite a few difficulties or problems you are flourishing and happy. What do you see? What are you doing? What are your kids doing? How is your life different from now, and what do you need to do to make this happen?

Michael and Anna felt they were stuck on a treadmill, both working in very demanding full-time jobs and raising two primary school-aged children. The couple were constantly tired and often grumpy with one another and with the children when they all spent time together on the weekend. They decided to create a life plan in order to achieve some clarity. They wrote a list of what they valued most. At the top of the list was quality family time, which was the very thing in short supply in their lives. They decided to make some changes. Michael, who had worked steadily through the young-baby phase, negotiated a nine-day fortnight with his employer and took a drop in salary. In order to afford this, they drew up a household budget, cutting out some of the extras such as regular takeaway and expensive gym memberships. Both were interested in gardening, so they decided to get the kids involved in planting a vegetable garden. This reduced their household expenses even further and gave them a family project to focus on. They scheduled in other regular family activities, such as a weekly movie night at home and once-a-month bushwalk. With this one big change (Michael's cut in working hours), and a series of smaller changes, they gradually began to feel more in control of their family life, and happier as a result.

7. Prioritise and focus

Do you ever feel like you're constantly busy but not achieving anything important? Many working parents claim the resource they lack most is time, but, like all people, tend to spend their lives putting out spot fires – those constant requests, problems and demands that come down the phone line and land in our email inboxes throughout the day. Dr Stephen Covey, author of the bestseller *The 7 Habits of Highly Effective People*, drew a distinction between 'urgent' and 'important' activities. Urgent activities are the spot fires such as an annoying email from the firm's accountant demanding last month's budget. Important activities involve attending to the things in life that sustain us emotionally, intellectually, physically and spiritually. When we are sustained in this way, our children benefit. Not just from the extra amount of time and attention from their parents, but because their parents are happier, more balanced people.

Our willingness to react to seemingly urgent tasks means we focus more on our working life, where everything needs to be done yesterday, rather than our family life, where things more or less tick along from day to day. We end up feeling fractured, guilty and incomplete as a result. We know we are avoiding the things that really matter in life, but have no idea how to stop doing the 'urgent' tasks that sap our energy and demand our attention.

Good intentions are not enough to change this sort of behaviour. You need to structure your time in quite a formalised way, at least to begin with. Set aside an hour each week. Block it out in your diary. Turn off your email and silence your phone. List all the urgent tasks you need to attend to, work or non-work, and then create another list of the things in your life that are most important to you. This second list might include:

- the children's education and general wellbeing
- your partner's happiness
- time with friends
- getting fit
- more sustaining and interesting work.

Arrange your diary accordingly, blocking out time for important activities alongside the urgent tasks. Your entries for important activities might look something like this:

- one hour, two evenings a week, helping the children with homework
- an afternoon on the weekend spent outdoors with the whole family
- an evening out with your partner
- one hour to call two friends who have been out of touch for a while
- three one-hour blocks for exercise
- two hours investigating options for study that could lead to more interesting job opportunities.

At the end of each week, check back over your diary. Make a note of whether or not you managed to achieve what you set out to do, and of the things that interfered with your attempt to stick to your schedule. Then begin planning for the next week.

8. Recognise negative thoughts

The next three chapters show you how to recognise, categorise and manage negative thoughts in all areas of your life, but particularly as a parent. Having these skills will ensure your children benefit in both the short and long term: they will come to know the joy of living with parents who cope with difficult situations effectively, and will learn and eventually develop good personal coping strategies for themselves through the power of their parents' modelling. For parents who actively want to involve their children now in managing negative thoughts, see page 20.

But first off, how do we come to recognise a negative thought? A good way is to simply write it down as it occurs.

Begin by writing a brief description of the situation. Where were you? What were you doing? Who were you with? Just a few words for each will do.

Next, write down what mood you were in and what emotions you were experiencing, such as sadness, anxiety, stress, worry, guilt, anger or frustration, or any combination of these.

Write down the thoughts that were going through your mind at the time. What was it about that situation that upset you? What did it mean to you when someone did or said a particular thing? Be as comprehensive as possible.

Assess whether each thought or interpretation was helpful. There are not necessarily 'right' or 'wrong' ways of thinking, but there are thoughts and interpretations that are not productive in some situations. For example, your child comes home from school and says her friend was mean to her. You jump to the conclusion that this could indicate your child is being bullied. You worry all night about the consequences. Here are some alternative explanations: your child said something mean first, prompting a response; your child exaggerated to get a bit of attention from Mum or Dad; your child remembers only the negative bit and forgot to tell you they made up later and are now best friends.

The aim of this exercise is to remind you that there are always different ways of looking at things, and some ways offer a greater prospect of peace and happiness than others.

9. Categorise negative thoughts

Read the previous chapter for how to first recognise negative thoughts (see page 15) and the next on how to manage these thoughts (see page 20). This chapter shows you how to actively categorise or label these thoughts as they occur.

Over the past few decades, clinical psychologists and researchers have identified a number of common 'thinking mistakes'. Giving these mistakes a name can make it easier to recognise them.

Here is a list of the ten most frequent thinking mistakes. Do any sound familiar to you?

Overgeneralisation: Coming to a general conclusion based on a single event or piece of evidence; expecting bad things to happen again and again even if they have only happened once.

> *Example: 'Harry screamed in the supermarket. He's always throwing tantrums.'*

Filtering: Concentrating on the negatives while ignoring the positives; ignoring important information that contradicts your (negative) view of a situation.

> *Example: 'Julie only got eight out of ten in her test. I don't know how she could have made those two mistakes.'*

All-or-nothing thinking: Viewing situations at the extremes with no middle ground.

> *Example: 'The kids always fight, so there's no point taking them out to dinner.'*

Personalising: Thinking that what people say or do is some kind of reaction to you, or is in some way related to you; taking responsibility for something that's not your fault.

> *Example: 'My five-year-old son always seems to be fighting; I must be a terrible parent.'*

Catastrophising: Overestimating the chances of disaster; expecting something unbearable or intolerable to happen.

> *Example: 'What if my kids fall off the play equipment and hurt themselves?'*

Emotional reasoning: Mistaking feelings for facts; believing that negative things you feel about yourself are true because they feel true.

> *Example: 'Parenting feels so hard; I must be hopeless at it.'*

Mind-reading: Making assumptions about other people's thoughts, feelings and behaviours without checking the evidence.

> *Example: 'My wife and I often disagree about the kids; she must think I'm a terrible father.'*

Fortune-telling: Anticipating an outcome and assuming your prediction is an established fact.

> *Example: 'My son's always going to be a troublemaker.'*

'Should' statements: Using 'should', 'ought', or 'must' statements that set up unrealistic expectations of yourself and others; operating by rigid rules and not allowing for flexibility.

> *Example: 'My kids should be able to play sport as well as I can.'*

Magnification/minimisation: Exaggerating the importance of negative information or experiences, while trivialising positive information or experiences.

> *Example: 'Saying sorry to my daughter doesn't compensate for that time last week when I yelled at her.'*

If any of these thoughts are part of your thinking pattern, don't despair. We can all make these mistakes, especially during times of stress. The most important thing is to determine whether these mistakes are adversely affecting your life, and whether you're prepared to work hard at correcting them.

Next time you go into a phase of negative thinking, note down the thought, as described in the previous chapter, then analyse that thought using the list opposite. For example, you child comes home with a bad grade. Do you:

- Overgeneralise: 'This always happens'?
- Fortune tell: 'My child has no future'?
- Personalise: 'This is completely my fault'?

Being able to label the thought as it occurs automatically creates a sense of perspective. You'll start to recognise your tendencies, which will help you with the next step in the process – managing your thoughts (see page 20).

10. Manage negative thoughts

Once you have learnt how to recognise negative thoughts (see page 15) and to categorise or label them (see page 17) you are in a good position to start actively challenging and managing these thoughts.

The easiest way to do this is to list your thoughts, and ask yourself a series of questions relating to these thoughts.

Say for example your thirteen-year-old daughter is caught shoplifting. Your first thoughts are very negative:

- 'She's headed for a life of crime.'
- 'I've been a lousy parent.'
- 'She has no self-control.'
- 'Her friends are awful.'
- 'If this is the start of some really bad teen behaviour, I will never cope.'

You could then ask yourself a series of questions that test these assumptions:

- 'How often has she been in this kind of trouble?'
- 'What other evidence is there that I have been a bad parent?'
- 'Are there some recent examples of my child doing really well or taking on a project that requires a lot of discipline and focus?'
- 'Who is she hanging around with at the moment? Of her peers, who do I like/dislike and why?'
- Have I experienced other situations with my kids that have put a lot of pressure on my ability to cope?'

Your answers may surprise you. In this situation, they might look something like this:

- My daughter was in trouble just once before for damaging school property, but she was remorseful and willing to accept punishment.
- My other kids are great. My parenting style has worked well generally – there have been no other instances of this kind in the family. This particular child is a bit of a rebel, or is just going through a phase.
- The flipside of my daughter's rebellious personality is that she often thinks of new and interesting ways of doing things. Her teachers say she always contributes to debates in a lively way and she is very creative and focused when doing art and drama projects.
- Her choice of friends has generally been good. Lately she has been hanging around with a couple of kids who are a little troubled, but she can and does think for herself in friendship situations – she is not a follower.
- I have experienced a couple of tough times with the kids, particularly when my youngest was sick as a small baby. We coped with this very well as a family. I am sure we will cope with this new situation in a positive and resourceful way.

Try this a few times, even with quite low-key situations, and you will see how effective and empowering this process is.

Carmel found a novel way to deal with fairly high levels of anxiety. While in therapy, she came to understand and embrace the idea that there are always different ways of looking at a situation. She developed an exercise where she imagined that her thoughts were like index cards that occasionally popped up in response to certain triggers. She also imagined that if she did not like a particular card she could tap it back down and select another card. This way she always had a number of 'thought cards' to choose from and would endeavour to choose the one that enabled her to make a positive assessment of things in whatever situation she found herself.

11. Recognise your strengths

Too many people spend too much time trying to fix their problems and shortcomings instead of focusing on their strengths. In contrast, working with your strengths is easy, energising and enjoyable. Once you know how to do this, it will be easy for you to work with your kids on encouraging them to identify their particular strengths (see page 44).

Remember that none of us is, or ever will be, perfect; the best we can do is make the most of our qualities and skills. One of the chief proponents of positive psychology, Martin Seligman, along with his colleagues, developed the following list of personal strengths. These are not talents or skills, but rather personal qualities. Most of us will be strong in about five or six areas. Run through this list and think about each category. You will know if you have a particular strength if you imagine yourself doing a particular task associated with that strength, and you get a sense of yourself as being in control, engaged, happy and productive. So, for example, a task associated with bravery may involve volunteering for the community fire service. A task associated with citizenship may involve putting up your hand to serve on the parent council at your local school. If these actions feel natural, rewarding and pleasing, then you are working in an area of strength. The more we work in our areas of strength, the happier we are. Try these on for size:

appreciation of beauty and excellence	citizenship	diligence
	creativity	discretion
bravery	critical thinking	empathy
caution	curiosity	energy

enthusiasm	integrity	perspective
equity	judgement	playfulness
fairness	kindness	practical intelligence
faith	leadership	prudence
forgiveness	love of learning	self-control
generosity	loyalty	sense of purpose
gratitude	mercy	social awareness
honesty	modesty	spirituality
hope	open-mindedness	sympathy
humility	optimism	teamwork
humour	originality	valour
industry	passion	vitality
ingenuity	perseverance	zest

Go to authentichappiness.sas.upenn.edu for a questionnaire that helps you identify your strengths. The following chapter shows you how to utilise these strengths.

12. Utilise your strengths

Now that you have used the list on pages 23–24 to identify your strengths, the challenge is to work out how to utilise them as often as possible. Here are some examples:

- If you value beauty, volunteer at an art gallery or keep a journal of inspirational things.
- If curiosity is your strength, read a book or attend a lecture on a topic you know nothing about, or go to a restaurant that specialises in a cuisine unfamiliar to you.
- If you believe you find it easy to be grateful, write and send a letter to someone who deserves to be thanked.
- If kindness is your strength, think about a career working with children or sick or elderly people, or offer to volunteer in this capacity.
- If you're a leader, take responsibility for an unpleasant task at work and make sure that it gets done.

Don't underplay your strengths – this is a very common mistake, partly because when we are working with our strengths things feel easy rather than hard. Many people tend to focus on perfecting areas of weakness. While this can be important, it can also make you feel as if you are constantly on the back foot. When you work with your strengths you build confidence, and this confidence provides a solid foundation for happiness in all areas of life.

When asked, Maria struggled to identify any strengths she brought to the task of parenting. She rarely felt confident. When she came to see me as a patient, I asked her to describe a time when she enjoyed being with her children, or believed her children enjoyed being with her. She thought for a moment and spoke of the times she talked to her ten-year-old son about 'life, the universe and everything'. She noted that often, when preparing dinner for her children, she would chat and philosophise with her son and debate all manner of issues and topics. When I asked her why she had not immediately recognised this as a parenting strength she said she thought she probably should spend more time with him kicking a ball around the park (something she disliked and didn't feel she was very good at).

13. Plant optimistic thoughts

As well as challenging and managing negative thoughts (see page 20), it is important to develop optimistic, constructive and helpful thoughts. I'm not just talking about thoughts that will help you overcome distress or deal with particular situations, but thoughts that will help you experience an ongoing sense of achievement and happiness.

The key is to develop a flexible, positive attitude. Begin by asking yourself general questions such as:

- What are my best qualities?
- Who and what are the best things in my life?
- What good and great things are happening in the world?
- What can I look forward to in the future?
- What did I achieve today?
- What am I going to achieve tomorrow?
- What progress have I made and what am I doing to achieve even more progress?

Then focus on your specific situation, with questions such as:

- What's the best thing about this situation?
- What positives can I take from this situation?
- What can I learn from this and how can I be better as a result?

If you're not used to focusing on these themes or saying positive things about yourself, you might initially find this awkward or difficult. Don't worry; this is a skill that requires practice. Remember that with mastery of positive thinking comes enhanced happiness. To help you get used to planting optimistic thoughts, try the following optimism exercise.

For two weeks before you go to bed write down three to five positive things that happened that day. Reflect on how happy they made you feel. Or write down three to five things for which you are grateful. Think how good it will be to look back on this record.

14. Understand the importance of optimism

I'm often asked, 'What's the secret to happiness?' The truth is there isn't one. There's not one thing that will make every single person reading this book happy – if there was, we all would have worked it out by now.

That said, if I had to pick one element that can strongly influence your chances of happiness, it would be optimism. Optimism, or positive thinking, can be learned, and learning to think positively can enhance your happiness and improve your health, the quality of your relationships and your performance in the workplace.

A wonderful example of the power of positive thinking is Roger Bannister, the first athlete to break the four-minute mile. Athletes had been trying to break the four-minute barrier for years, and many experts of the day (athletes, coaches and doctors) believed that it was impossible, that the human body was not physically advanced enough. Bannister proved them wrong: in May 1954 he ran a mile in just over three minutes and fifty-nine seconds.

To me, the most amazing part of this story is not Bannister's incredible achievement but the fact that within the next six months many other athletes broke the four-minute barrier, including Australia's John Landy.

Why did all these athletes suddenly become capable of achieving something they once considered impossible? Because they believed they could do it. They thought, 'If he can do it, maybe I can too.'

If you believe you can achieve something, then as long as that belief is realistic – I'm not talking about blind faith or unrealistic optimism, which can be unhelpful, dangerous and self-defeating – you will achieve it; if you believe you can perform and succeed and be happy then you significantly increase your chances of realising these goals.

15. Foster healthy relationships – you and your partner

The quality of your relationship with your partner plays a significant role in your overall happiness and wellbeing. A high-quality relationship provides a buffer against stress, depression and other negative emotions, and promotes a positive sense of wellbeing, which in turn helps you be a better parent (see page 31 for tips on promoting a positive relationship with your child). It may seem obvious, but one of the key elements of a positive relationship is support. This involves recognising and appreciating your partner's strengths, giving praise and positive feedback and maintaining open communication lines, respect and trust.

Try this exercise with your partner:

- Both make a list of all the things you'd like the other person to do for you, adding next to each entry a score from 0 to 100 reflecting how much pleasure you would get if your partner actually did these things.
- Swap lists and review your partner's tasks, then score them from 0 to 100 in relation to how much pain it would cause you to actually do each task.
- Compare the two scores: subtract the 'pain' score from the 'pleasure' score to give a final score. The items with the highest scores are the ones that will give the greatest pleasure for the least pain, so you both win. Start with the highest scores and work your way down the list.

16. Foster healthy relationships – you and your child

Recognising and appreciating your child's strengths and keeping communication lines open are vital aspects of nurturing and maintaining a quality relationship with your child, which will increase happiness for your whole family.

Try the following exercises with your child to promote a positive, rewarding relationship:

- Write them a letter expressing your gratitude for all the wonderful things they do: it could be that they make an effort to help around the house; they look after younger siblings; they are a good and kind friend at school. I know writing letters seems a bit old-fashioned, but I think this makes them even more powerful. Make time to give them the letter in person.
- Get involved with something your child is passionate about – it could be a book they're reading or bike riding or a charity they feel strongly about. If you can't do the activity with them, ask them about it and read up on it. Having connection points with your kids will show them you are interested in their life beyond the day-to-day routine.

17. Communicate effectively

If you need to discuss a complex or potentially distressing issue, timing is important. Try to find a time when you won't be rushed, tired or interrupted. Run through what you would like to say and how you would like to say it in your mind. Even better, say it aloud.

Effective communication is a two-way process, so remember to listen. If you are relaxed you will be in a better position to hear what the other person is saying and to say what you want to say. Be as specific as possible, and focus on actual behaviours. What was it about the situation that upset you? What did you or the other person do? What would you like the other person to do?

Remember that everyone has their own ideas about the way things *should* be done, so choose your words wisely. Rather than saying, 'This is how it should be,' use statements such as, 'I would like —' followed by a description of a specific behaviour. Try not to blame the other person by saying things like, 'You make me feel —'; instead say something like, 'When you did — I felt —'

Andrew found himself in constant battle with his teenage daughter, Sarah. She ignored curfews, dressed inappropriately for school and didn't complete homework. Their discussions on these issues usually ended in shouting matches. Andrew decided to try a different communication approach. Reminding himself to practise patience, he sat down with Sarah twice a week, just the two of them. He would ask Sarah how school was going and how her friends were. At first, Sarah blocked his attempts to communicate, but gradually she relaxed when she saw her dad was not going to yell or criticise her. Soon Andrew felt confident enough to start talking about why he was unhappy with some of Sarah's behaviour. He used language such as, 'When you come home late, your mother and I get very worried. We want you to enjoy yourself, but we want you to be safe as well.' Sarah felt she was being consulted and spoken to with respect. She started to trust her dad again, and slowly started to take on board some of his concerns.

18. Promote a healthy home and be a healthy role model

It's hard to be happy if you're sick and don't have the energy to do the things you want to do. Healthy living is essential to our sense of wellbeing, of which happiness is a crucial component, so it is important to be as active and healthy as possible.

I'm not an expert on health, fitness or weight loss, but I want to encourage you to promote a healthy, mindful home for yourself and your child. Make sure everyone in the family gets enough sleep, eats well and exercises regularly.

As with the other advice in this section, the more you focus on fixing things in your own life, the more effective you will be as a parent. Work with your strengths to do this. Here are some examples:

- If you embrace spirituality in your life, take up yoga or meditation.
- If you are strong on teamwork, organise a weekly team sport with other interested adults, or with another couple of families.
- If you have lots of practical intelligence, think about a family camping trip.
- If you are creative, become a whiz in the kitchen, cooking healthy, tasty meals for the family.

(See Section Five, from page 127, for more detailed information.)

19. Be mindful – enjoy the moment

How many times have you said to yourself, 'I'll be happy when I have more money/when I have a better job/when the kids leave home'? It's common to fall into this 'when' trap, but it's neither helpful nor conducive to happiness because it distracts us from the present and forces us to focus on a future that may never happen – or if it does happen it may be a disappointment.

Happiness tends to be experienced more as part of a process, rather than the achievement of an ultimate goal or the attainment of a particular object. Positive emotions attached to material possessions are short-lived; put simply, we get used to things, so what's new and special today is simply the norm tomorrow. That's not to say that material possessions are bad for you; just that if you look towards 'stuff' as a means of finding happiness you'll constantly be disappointed.

Happy people live in the present rather than dwell on the past or worry about the future. We can learn from the past but we can't change it, just like we can plan for the future but worrying about it won't make it turn out the way we want.

Living in the moment is something that most kids are naturally great at. Although it can be frustrating for parents at times – such as when you're in a hurry to get them out the door but they're only interested in playing with whatever they're playing with or watching whatever they're watching – what they're often doing is simply enjoying the here and now. They don't realise you need to be somewhere in twenty minutes and they don't really care, because (depending on their age, of course) they have little concept of the future.

Set aside ten minutes every day to consciously focus on whatever activity is at hand – whether it's washing the dishes, walking your kids to school, or sharing a family meal. Every time your mind wanders to past or future events, bring it back to the now. If you do this regularly, and increase the number of times you do it during the day, you will start to notice a marked shift in your attention. You will complete tasks in a more satisfying and fulfilling way, and feel altogether calmer and more in control.

20. Learn from your children – play and have fun

Our children learn from us every day, but what lessons can they teach us? The most important is how to have fun. It seems almost too obvious to say, but happiness, while not solely dependent on pleasure, is closely linked.

Many of us are so focused on our parenting, our jobs, our mortgages we forget to have any fun at all.

Next time you are out and about with your kids, make a point of looking at the things that entertain them. Very small children will take delight at the simplest of things, for example, the canopy of trees they can see from their pram. Older kids will light up when they see a friend, hop on a bike or embark on a game of backyard cricket.

Make a point of sharing your child's moment of fun, but also make time for some adult fun, such as:

- going out to dinner with your partner
- joining a book club
- having lunch with a friend
- taking up some new and exciting activity like kayaking or sailing.

Adults have an amazing ability to overcomplicate things, and often we imagine life is far more difficult than it needs to be. Being happy doesn't result from solving the world's problems; it's a state of mind with which you confront the world's problems.

Section Two

20 ways to build character

Character is a word that is not used as frequently as it was a generation or two ago. These days the focus is more on achievement, for both children and adults. You will often hear a parent talking about their child's good grades or sporting performance, but you are less likely to hear them discuss their child's positive outlook or sense of fair play. Achievement is something that can be measured, but character and its building blocks – resilience, courage, humour, flexible thinking and compassion – are less tangible and often develop and mature over a long period of time. This chapter talks about how to recognise and encourage the qualities associated with character. It also discusses how this will not only help your child with their day-to-day activities (and sense of achievement), but how it will provide the tools for coping with some of life's more challenging situations.

21. The different stages of development – for you and your child

There are no right or wrong ways to parent your child, but the following guidelines may help you think about how you will approach each stage of your child's life:

- In your child's early years, up to the age of about eight, your role is most likely to be one of teacher. During these early years your child learns what's right and wrong, how things work and what they can and cannot do.
- During your child's next phase, up to and during adolescence, you will shift into more of a coaching role. As often as possible, try to help your child review all available options, consider the consequences of different alternatives and then make their own decisions.
- Finally, as your child moves from late adolescence to early adulthood you will gradually take on a mentoring role. Share experiences about what has and hasn't worked for you in the past to help your child make their decisions.

Of course these stages should not be considered distinct or mutually exclusive, but rather approaches that can be blended as appropriate. Thinking in this way will assist you in your role, and help your child develop and become their own person.

Eliza has two girls, fourteen-year-old Kaz and seven-year-old Nita. She has not always found it easy to deal with this large age gap, particularly on issues to do with discipline. In the interests of fairness, she has had one set of rules for both children, but this has caused difficulty – too much freedom for the younger child and too little freedom for the older child. After a particularly difficult weekend of constant hassling over bedtimes, outings and screen time, she decided to try the suggestion of one of her friends who is a teacher, and adopt a different parenting approach with each child. At first it was difficult, but after some false starts she got the hang of it. With her younger child, Nita, Eliza now gets actively involved with many issues. She does not offer a string of choices, as she once did, and gives Nita clear directions for homework and other daily routines. She offers lots of explanations and encouragement, and is not afraid to say a simple 'no' to activities she considers age inappropriate. With Kaz, Eliza has taken a more consultative approach. She does not jump in to help with homework as soon as her daughter struggles, but encourages her to work through the problem. She is willing to negotiate, particularly on issues to do with her daughter's social life, and makes a point of asking Kaz for her opinion on issues that affect the whole family. If Kaz has a problem with a friendship, Eliza does not immediately offer a solution, but instead she asks a series of questions that encourage Kaz to draw her own conclusions. The children have adapted to this change, and Eliza now feels much more effective in her parenting.

22. Use Socratic questioning

The Greek philosopher Socrates was famous for teaching not through didactic means but through the posing of subtle, carefully worded questions. His premise was that students will learn more effectively if they come up with the answers themselves.

This approach has been refined and modified over the years, but the basic elements of Socratic questioning are still considered among the most effective strategies for changing thoughts and beliefs. If you accept that your thoughts may not be helpful or realistic, question them. This is a very effective way of developing more useful ways of thinking that can lead to greater happiness and success.

This approach is especially valuable for children, and an effective way for you to help them form their own opinions. It also helps you understand your child's position, which is a crucial step in communicating and assisting. Phrase your questions in a way to gently guide your child towards a sensible and appropriate answer or solution. Try to avoid 'Why?' questions; instead, consider the following:

- What is it about this that —?
- What do you think you can do about this?
- What options are available?
- Is there another way of thinking about this?
- To what extent do you think —?
- What evidence do you have for this?

23. Recognise, challenge and manage negative thoughts in your child

In Section One we discussed recognising, categorising and managing your thoughts (see pages 15–22). Now you know a little bit more about the ways to deal with them (and hopefully these methods are working for you), start looking out for negative thoughts in your child. We all know kids can be negative now and then, but when it starts to become a regular pattern, there is cause for concern. Use the exercises from Section One to help your child see the other side of the situation, and encourage them to look at all angles. Weave in some Socratic questioning too (see opposite).

Jeanie and Doug's daughter, Annie, often came home from school with 'woe is me' stories. Nothing had gone right, friends were being mean, teachers picked on her, she didn't make the netball team. Her parents knew things had to change. First, they checked with Annie's teacher to make sure everything was actually okay. Having confirmed that Annie seemed to be doing well and had some good solid friendships, her parents decided on the following approach. Whenever their daughter started to get negative about school, they asked her to write down three good things that had happened that day. It was a simple exercise, but it seemed to slowly turn the situation around. Within a few weeks Annie was volunteering information about the good things that had happened that day, and if something had gone wrong she tended to brush it off and move on quickly.

24. Help your child recognise their strengths

Depending on their age, you should have a fairly good idea of what your child is good at and what they enjoy, but remember to ask them too!

My own two children are extremely different, and it took my wife and me some time to realise where their personal strengths lie. My daughter Tali likes to review all her options thoroughly before making her choice. My son Coby, however, typically chooses the first thing he sets his eyes on, which can be easier from our perspective (especially if we're in a hurry) but can also cause problems – and regrets – down the track. We now remind ourselves that our children are simply using their strengths – Tali's include caution and self-control; Coby's include energy, zest and vitality.

Review the list of signature strengths on pages 23–24, and consider how each might be perceived in a positive and negative light in relation to your child, then create a list of your child's personal signature strengths.

Then look at your reactions – and the reaction of other adults – to aspects of your child's behaviour. Are there things that annoy you, and, if so, could these be cast in a more positive light. For example:

- Your child is extremely sensitive and is often being told to toughen up. This could mean your child is very strong on empathy and able to thrive in situations where care and consideration are important and valued qualities.
- Your child is stubborn and argues the point constantly. She is often told by you and her teachers to 'move on', or 'get over it'. This could mean that your child has high perseverance and is willing to always go the extra distance for what she believes is right.

- Your child is always asking questions. It can be annoying. Sometimes you think that he is just not getting certain things. But it could also be that he is naturally curious, and that this curiosity will lead him to explore the world in a way that will present wonderful opportunities further down the track.

Take the time to challenge your thoughts about your child as they arise, and make an effort to turn a negative interpretation of your child's behaviour into a positive one – like this:

- **Original thought:** my child seems to take an age to make decisions; she should be able to choose something more quickly.
- **New thought:** my child is, in reality, highly discretionary and cautious, strengths that will hold her in good stead in many situations.

Talk to your child about their strengths but be careful not to pigeonhole them. Remind them that as they grow they may develop new strengths to complement the ones that come naturally to them. For example, high levels of creativity may need to be balanced by industry and perseverance, just as caution may need to be counterbalanced with courage.

25. Help your child build on their strengths

Once you've recognised your child's strengths help them make the most of them by putting them to use in areas of interest. For example, if your child is diligent and cautious give her the task of adding up the grocery bill while you shop, or let her help with the family budget. Or if your son is energetic and has great hand–eye coordination give him balls and bats to play with rather than sitting him at a table with crayons and paper. Of course, all these activities are part of growing up, but be conscious of pushing your child into things *you* want them to do rather than things *they* want to do.

We all know people (and are envious of them!) who truly love their job because they work with their strengths in a field in which they are interested. Surely that's the kind of life experience we want our kids to have too.

Consider the following points when you help your child build on their strengths:

- Is it what *they* want to do, or what *you* want them to do?
- Are they enjoying the challenge and making progress?
- Do they feel a sense of achievement?
- Are there areas in which they have an interest but not necessarily the right skills? If so, help them gain those skills.

26. Guide your child

Now that you're equipped to help your child recognise and build on their strengths (see pages 44–46) and start thinking for themselves, be prepared for a new journey.

Of course, it's important your child doesn't feel as though they are being lead or pushed into a position, but at the same time your aim should be to gently and helpfully guide them in the right direction.

When your child comes across a situation they need help with work with them to clarify the exact nature of the problem or issue; ensure that all options for action have been explored; assess the pros and cons of each option, including short- and long-term consequences; and determine a reasonable course of action or a best decision.

Of course this takes longer than simply telling your child what they 'should' do, but ultimately this is time well spent because your child will learn to think through their own issues and eventually become less dependent on you for answers.

> Jenna is thirteen years old. She was accepted into the school concert band a few months ago as a clarinet player. At first she was really excited, but is now bored. She says that they never play anything interesting, and that the teacher is dull. Jenna's mother Mia wants Jenna to stick with it. After all they have paid the fees for the music program. But instead of insisting, she decides to sit down with Jenna to work things out. Mia, with careful questioning, finds out that the teacher is a bit of a drill master and very focused on performance rather than process. Jenna is a good player and very creative – rehearsals

are not giving her anything she hasn't already got. Mia acknowledges Jenna's frustration, and between them they work out a compromise. Jenna will stick with it until the end of the term, and then swap to the jazz band, which is led by a young, exciting teacher. Mia points out that this will cost extra and she expects Jenna to stick with the jazz band for at least one year.

27. Be kind to one another

It's great for your kids to be able to make decisions for themselves, but they also need to know that sometimes other people's feelings and needs are involved. Be clear about the type of behaviours you would like to see in them, especially in relation to others. For example, reward not only their good behaviour but also kind, considerate treatment of others, including siblings, classmates and even you!

Once they understand these positive behaviours and how pleased you are with them, continue to reinforce them. Praise them when they succeed; if they miss the mark remind them of the type of behaviour you prefer.

28. Define right and wrong

Children aren't born with an in-built moral compass; we need to teach them what's right and wrong. Helping your child understand what's important is one of the most challenging tasks you will face as a parent, but it should also be one of your highest priorities. You play a major role in teaching your child the value of health, relationships, education, diligence, working towards long-term goals, patience and tolerance.

I believe that the most effective way to achieve this is by modelling appropriate behaviours and attitudes (see page 6). For example, it would be incredibly hard for any child to understand how to save money when their parents spend excessively, how to be active when their parents live a predominantly sedentary life, or how to show respect when their parents swear at or abuse one another.

Another key strategy in teaching your child values is open discussion – this will help them fully understand the underlying principles in order to live and breathe them. When they're young, this can be done by reading them children's books and then discussing the key messages together. I like to think of reading to my children as an interactive activity and one that easily leads to some of the more fascinating and enlightening discussions, including chats about what's right and wrong.

29. Help your child develop purpose and define goals

Helping your child define clear goals, values and priorities is an incredibly valuable service you can provide. As well as setting them on the path to learning right from wrong (see page 50) it's essential to help your child clarify what is important – and, just as significantly, what is not. This will help them determine how, when and where they set their goals, now and in the future.

Encourage your child to consider things that are important to you, such as in the following examples:

- If you value the environment encourage your child to help out with recycling at home and in your neighbourhood.
- If you value equality ensure it is reflected in your interactions at home as well as your discussions about work, news and current affairs (depending, of course, on your child's age).
- If you value healthy living encourage the whole family to eat well and exercise regularly.
- If you value education watch less mindless TV, read more and encourage your child to do the same; actively participate in their homework; when they ask questions, search for the answers collaboratively with them.

Encourage and assist your child in their attempts to become involved in relevant activities. Positive reinforcement makes it easier and more enjoyable for them to get involved in what you and they have determined to be priorities. This support should be gradually scaled back over time, but the more you can help your child when they're starting out, the more likely they are to succeed and be happy.

Every June long weekend, the Bond family works together to create a collage. As they browse through magazines for pictures, they play their favourite CDs, which leads to singing and dancing. Everyone loves the experience. There is no right or wrong – if someone likes an image, it goes in. The collage is displayed and throughout the year the Bond family talks about it. They are often amazed at how the images seem to reflect events that unfold during the year.

30. Set clear goals

The key to setting clear goals is to be smart about them: make sure they're easily integrated into your child's life and are clearly defined within an achievable time frame.

For example, if your child would like a new game, book or toy, goal setting fits perfectly within a savings plan. If your child would love to play a particular sport or musical instrument, goal setting can be used to help encourage them to practise regularly in order to achieve certain outcomes – getting a place on the school team or learning a new tune.

Where appropriate, discuss and share with your child your own experience of goal setting and how you use it to achieve what you want to achieve at work or in relation to your hobbies.

There are countless examples of how famous and successful people have started small and built up their success or achievements. Finding an appropriate role model your child is interested in learning from can also be a powerful and effective way to teach these principles.

31. Encourage realistic expectations

Real and meaningful happiness is fundamentally dependent on having realistic expectations of what life will hold. Accordingly, we all need to face the reality that bad things happen and things go wrong; we have all faced adversity at some stage in our lives and so will our children.

It's good to dream and set goals, but ups and downs are inevitable so it's vital to equip your child with the skills to accept, evaluate and push on. When explaining a situation that hasn't worked out as intended be calm, be fair and give your child as much information as possible as to why the result differed from what you'd planned or hoped for.

Encourage your child to try new things, even if they don't think they'll be able to do them (or do them perfectly). This principle is illustrated beautifully in a wonderful book entitled *Ish* by Peter Reynolds. The main character likes to draw, until the day his brother laughs at one of his pictures. As a result he gives up his artistic endeavours because the objects of his efforts do not look like they're supposed to. He then discovers that his younger sister loves his work and has been collecting his discards. When he asks why she likes them she responds, in reference to a drawing of a vase, that it looks 'vase-ish'. He then comes to realise that all his pictures look 'something-ish' and that perfection is clearly not the goal of drawing. He comes to understand that simply trying to capture an image as 'ish' as possible can still be enjoyable and fulfilling.

32. Build resilience

Truly happy people take pleasure when things are good, and cope well when they're not. Have you ever noticed that people who have what's referred to as 'authentic happiness' quickly bounce back from adversity? Happy people are resilient, and not surprisingly, resilience breeds happiness.

As a parent, and as a professional who's determined to do what I can to promote happiness and positivity, I can think of few things I'd consider more important than building resilience in our children.

Building resilience in young people improves their social and emotional functioning, which will in turn significantly reduce their chances of experiencing psychological difficulties later in life such as stress, anxiety, relationship problems and depression, and turning to ineffective and damaging coping strategies such as drugs and alcohol.

Resilient children are ones who can make decisions, resist pressure and act independently. The following exercises will help build these strengths:

- When you have the time, give younger children a choice – this might include what to wear, what not to wear, where to go for a walk. Offering them two or three options is a good idea.
- Again with younger children, think of a useful task that will allow your child to experience a sense of mastery. When you are gardening get your child to water the plants. If you are tidying the kitchen they can help by putting away containers in the right cupboard or drawer.
- With older children, it's a good idea to get them thinking about problem solving ahead of the problem actually occurring. You can

turn this into a thought game over dinner or while driving with questions like:

- ° What would you do if someone at school was being bullied?
- ° Imagine one teacher wanted you to fill in for someone in the choir at a performance but another wanted you to finish off a project on the same night. What would you do?
- ° What would you say to a friend who dared you to jump in the water off the rocks at the beach even though there was a sign saying not to?

Keep up with your child as they grow. Their capacity for reflection and their need for mastery shifts all the time. By giving your child more and more challenging tasks, you are telling them you believe in their ability to handle a variety of situations with intelligence, competence and resilience.

33. Reinforce optimism and hope when things go wrong

There are helpful and unhelpful ways to interpret events, and, as parents, it is our job to help our children interpret what goes on around them in the most helpful, happiness-inducing way. Think about these three ways of interpreting events:

- permanent versus temporary
- general versus specific
- internal versus external.

People who are susceptible to depression interpret negative events in a permanent, general and internal way. They are convinced that the negative experience will last forever (permanent interpretation); that things always go wrong (general interpretation); and everything is their fault (internal interpretation).

By contrast, a person with a more positive outlook will tend to interpret events in a temporary, specific and external way. They know that the negative experience won't last forever (temporary interpretation); only one thing, not everything, has gone wrong (specific interpretation); and it's probably not their fault, but the fault of some outside circumstance (external interpretation).

As has been discussed elsewhere, we come into this world with a propensity towards either optimism or pessimism, but it is very much the case that we can learn to become more optimistic thinkers who deal with problems using the temporary/specific/external model. When it comes to our children, our best approach is to model optimism, to let them see us interpreting and coping with difficult events in the above way. Other than that, there are quite specific exercises we can do with our children to enhance their levels of optimism:

- Create a 'positive events diary': every evening ask your child to write three to five positive events that happened that day in a notebook.
- The 'gratitude diary' follows a similar routine: each day ask your child to list all the things in their life for which they are grateful.
- 'Positive reading' simply involves discussing books your child has read (or that you have read to them), focusing on the positive messages that come from the stories.
- Imagining and discussing with your child a 'hopeful future' is a great forward-thinking exercise in which you encourage your child to imagine the most beautiful and happy future life possible. Your role here is not to dampen their enthusiasm but to encourage and guide them to imagine as many positives as they can – and this exercise does not need to be grounded in reality at all!

34. Identify negative emotions

Many people meeting me for the first time want to know if I am happy *all* the time.

As humans we experience a whole gamut of emotions – positive and negative – and I passionately believe that part of our role as parents is to help our children first to understand *all* the varied emotions they might experience, and then to appropriately express and manage these feelings. In fact, the so-called 'negative emotions' don't need to be negative at all – we just need to use them as signs that something needs to be addressed or changed, and hopefully we're able to learn from them and improve in some way.

When my son asked me why I sometimes got angry with him if I was a 'happiness doctor', I saw the perfect opportunity to reinforce this point. I explained that everyone experiences negative emotions such as anger at times and that this was perfectly normal. The important thing is not that I might get angry from time to time but that I don't let my anger overtake me, that I don't express it violently or rudely and that I explain why I'm feeling the way I am to those involved. I emphasised that negative emotions are usually related to a specific behaviour rather than directed at a person. In other words, being angry with someone does not exclude loving them as a person at the same time.

35. Accept negative emotions

As I discussed on page 54, it is important to have realistic expectations of what life will hold – with this in mind, we must teach our children that their goal should not be to feel happy *all the time*; this unrealistic expectation will only lead to disappointment and frustration. Instead, the goal they (and we) should clarify and work towards is to feel happy *as often as possible* and to accept there will be times when they don't feel so good, and they can respond to and manage these times as best they can.

How do we help our children achieve this? One way is to consider how we typically respond to inappropriate expressions of distress and/or to inappropriate behaviours. In my experience, too many children are punished when they display distress and other forms of difficult behaviour. In most instances, tantrums, sulkiness and low-grades should simply be ignored, although parents must step in when a child becomes verbally and/or physically aggressive (see also page 62). Difficult be-haviour is often nothing more than an inappropriate way of getting attention. If the child is not rewarded, the behaviour will generally dissipate fairly quickly.

Carrie has five children aged eight to sixteen. Her friends always ask her how she manages. Carrie's response is that she focuses on the good things and tries not to pay a lot of attention to the moods, tears and dramas of daily life. Her first child was a big tantrum thrower as a toddler. Carrie would get upset and embarrassed by the behaviour and try to fix it. As each child came along, she began to see that this is what little children do when they are tired or frustrated. She started to refer to these moods as passing storms, and now the whole family does the same. When Carrie's sixteen year old slams a door, her younger son says, 'Low pressure system approaching.' Carrie also has a golden rule: 'Don't talk to the tantrum'. In other words, she won't try to argue with a child who is in full flight. She waits until they calm down before entering into any discussion. She has found this helps particularly in dealing with her teenagers – they have come to see that while it's okay to feel lousy a sulky or cross mood won't necessarily guarantee you a spot centre stage.

36. Manage negative emotions

Knowing and accepting that children will experience negative emotions does not mean we as parents need to accept *all* kinds of behaviour.

For example, if my son does not get something he wants it's not unreasonable that he might experience some degree of frustration or distress; what's not reasonable is for my son to yell and scream and hit people. The behaviour in this circumstance is unhelpful and only serves to exacerbate the situation, but that doesn't mean my son's initial emotional reaction was wrong.

There are all sorts of ways to help your child manage their emotions. With small children, you can use puzzles, books, pictures and music to explain different sorts of emotions, and to talk about how people express these emotions. Try the following with younger children:

- Dance to both happy and sad music, then talk about the difference.
- Look at pictures of faces showing different kinds of emotions.
- Do puzzles together, and notice the point at which your child becomes frustrated. Show your child how to continue with the puzzle, and talk about how everyone experiences difficult feelings at some time.
- Read stories such as *Where the Wild Things Are* by Maurice Sendak, a classic tale of a child going to bed 'without his supper' because he has been very rude to his mother, and of how he conquers his anger through his fantastical imaginings.

Older children are taught to manage negative emotions in school and through arranged activities such as sport. Team sports are particularly good for this. They provide a clear set of rules and the opportunity for children to learn that if, as players, they give way to their frustrations, they hold up the game and let down their team. Of course, this hasn't stopped many professional players from losing it on the field, but even those instances can be instructive. If you watch a game with your child, you can point out to them how individual players work to manage their anger and disappointment, and discuss what happens when they fail to do this successfully.

Of course, as with younger children, the best model is you. By all means, let your child see you angry, frustrated or sad, but let them also see you dealing with these moments in a mature and competent manner.

37. Equip your child with alternative response options

Sometimes we forget that children can't always regulate their emotions (neither, for that matter, can all adults). So when our children react to frustration or disappointment in a way we think is inappropriate, we might think it best to punish them, but unless we teach them alternative responses, they will never learn what else to do.

Here are some options to help your child come up with some better responses to negative emotions:

- Rather than screaming and yelling, your child can try slow breathing or a 'time out' (which should not just be seen as a punishment, but rather as a strategy for calming down and rethinking a situation).
- Rather than asking for something rudely, your child can say please or thank you.
- Rather than hitting another person, your child can phrase a request in a way that is more likely to achieve a good outcome without causing anyone harm.

Of course, encouraging these alternative responses is only half the process: you as the parent must also model appropriate behavioural responses for your child.

38. Encourage your child to find solutions to problems

Positive emotions help us think creatively about solutions to problems, lower the effects of stress and make it easier for us to withstand the tough times. Here are some concepts and ideas you can teach your child to help them deal with problems:

- Happy, resilient people don't always cope with everything on their own; they ask for help. Encourage your child to utilise their support network, which of course includes you.
- Help your child avoid dwelling on the past; instead teach them to learn from their experiences: reflect on what went well, what didn't go so well and what they might do differently if they had their time again. This should be approached in a supportive, positive way rather than with criticism.
- Teach your child that change is inevitable and is an opportunity to improve and benefit.
- Remind your child not to lose sight of their goals, and that it's okay to fall over, as long as they get up again. Teach your child that very few people achieve success without experiencing failure, and failure should be viewed as just another part of the overall journey.
- Prompt your child to focus on what they *can* do rather than what they *can't* do in difficult situations.

39. Encourage perseverance

A problem most parents face is that of knowing how much to encourage their child in an activity they are finding difficult. This often arises when a child takes up an instrument or some other hobby or interest. It is important to remember that some of the things we need to do to have a better life might be difficult or uncomfortable at first, but in most cases if we practise these skills we will inevitably improve and gain more enjoyment from them!

Consider the following points when thinking about how to encourage your child to persevere:

- Are you encouraging them to do an activity that you like more than they like?
- Are they working with their strengths?
- If they are complaining of being bored, is there a way of making the activity more challenging?
- Is there a way of better organising practice time in order to improve skills and create a greater sense of mastery?
- Is there someone your child admires who could serve as a role model?
- Do you praise your child when they have a go? Are they getting enough reinforcement and encouragement?

Julian started playing soccer when he was eight years old. Many of his team mates had been playing for a couple of years and Julian felt he wasn't very good in comparison. He started saying he didn't want to go to soccer practice or matches because he didn't like soccer. His dad David asked Julian to give it one more month before he quit. A couple of times a week, David took Julian up to the park to practise soccer drills. Julian's skills developed and he started to feel more confident. Just before his month was up, Julian kicked a goal in a game. Of course, after that, there was no talk of quitting. David talked to Julian about how practice leads to achievement; he gently pointed out that if Julian had quit when he first wanted to he wouldn't have known what it felt like to achieve what he had.

40. Appreciate all forms of happiness

As parents, our aim is to raise happy children with realistic expectations and with an understanding of all the emotions they will experience throughout life.

Happiness means much more than just the experience of the obvious forms of positive emotion such as joy, pleasure and excitement; we need to recognise, reinforce and encourage our children to appreciate other healthy forms of happiness such as calm, contentment, satisfaction, love, passion and many others.

Happiness comes not only from the emotions we feel but from the sensations of positive experiences – the taste of a delicious piece of cake, the feel of a warm bath or the sounds of birds and the wind as you walk in a park. It is important to show our children how to savour these sensations by slowing down and fully appreciating the experience.

We are so busy these days that we often value speed over attention and mindfulness, and we can inadvertently pay more attention to the negative things that happen in a day than to the positive ones. It's positive emotions, however, that allow us to really enjoy a good experience.

To help your child slow down and really appreciate the pleasures of ordinary day-to-day life, try the following:

- Go food shopping together and choose some interesting ingredients, perhaps a fruit you don't normally buy or different bread. When you get home do a taste test. Talk about the flavour, texture and the aroma of the food.
- Cook a meal with your child from beginning to end. Talk about the ingredients and the cooking process. Share the meal as a family and

talk about how the different ingredients contributed to the overall flavour.

• Spend some time with a special toy. Ask your child what she likes about that particular toy. Talk about where it came from and what it feels like when she plays with it.

• Go for a walk and talk about all the different things you see. Discuss the weather: is it hot, cold, sticky, or windy? Notice the people you pass, and create stories with your child about where the people have come from or where they are going.

• Go to a gallery or museum and spend time with a few special pieces. Your child might like to take a notebook and pencil so he can draw what he sees. Ask him what he likes about a particular piece and how he imagines it was created. When you get home, ask your child if he wants to create something similar.

Section Three
20 ways to set positive boundaries

Getting the boundaries right is possibly one of the most difficult and important tasks involved in parenting. We want our children to feel they are part of our lives, to be able to express themselves and be clear about their wants and needs. At the same time, we know they need to learn to abide by rules and regulations as well as consider the needs and wants of others. Setting boundaries takes time. You need to be patient, present and persistent, and you also need to lead by example. The good news is that establishing clear boundaries and sensible rules will change the day-to-day engagement you have with your child. They will know what you expect of them, which will limit the need for constant instruction and rebuke. You will have richer conversations and greater enjoyment of one another's company.

41. Model appropriate behaviours and attitudes

I'm constantly surprised when I work with organisations that promote values of 'caring for their people' and 'work–life balance' and I find their senior executives and managers are still working after nine, ten or even eleven o'clock at night. What message do you think this sends to the employees?

Similarly, there are many parents who say that their children are their top priority, but they struggle to spend time with them – and when they do, they're thinking about other things such as work. I know, because I've been guilty of this many times!

Consistency is conducive to happiness and to raising happy children. The key is to decide on a specific set of values and then act out the corresponding behaviours to uphold your values.

Children are sponges, ready to soak up everything around them, so find ways to model your values as consistently as possible. Consider the following suggestions when modelling appropriate behaviours:

- If your child yells at you or others, instead of punishing them, encourage, suggest or model an alternative, less aggressive and more helpful response.
- Rather than punishing your child for not sharing their toys, help them negotiate with siblings or friends so they all find something to play with.
- Show your child what they can do right, rather than telling them what they have done wrong.

Libby is very close to her thirteen-year-old daughter Ruby. Libby works full time but has always been conscious of the need to make time for her daughter. At evening over dinner, they talk about Ruby's day at school – her friends, teachers, lessons, and other interesting things that happened. Ruby has struggled at school at different times, but Libby has made a point of remaining calm and constructive. She'll talk Ruby through mistakes then together they will work out how to approach a problem. As a single mother with virtually no extended family, Libby knows that she is it when it comes to Ruby's family role models. She is very aware that Ruby watches how she copes with difficult situations, such as money worries or a bad day at work. She lets Ruby know that these are temporary problems, likely to be sorted in a few days or week, not things to get upset about. As a consequence, Ruby has learnt to deal with issues confidently as they arise. Teachers and other parents often comment on Ruby's maturity, positive outlook and clear sense of herself.

42. Set structures and boundaries

A common mistake parents make is to not provide reasonable, consistent structure in their family life, which can lead to confusion and uncertainty. By structure I mean routines that children can rely on and clear enforceable consequences for difficult or careless behaviour (see page 77).

I love structure, but I also believe in moderation. I'm not suggesting we all obsess about controlling every aspect of our lives, but I do believe that children (and most adults) function and feel better when they feel secure and safe within a reasonable structure. The following example highlights this.

For a research experiment, investigators set up a family-picnic scenario with a number of families. The parents gathered in the middle of a large, open area and their children were encouraged to play and roam wherever they wanted to. Despite having no restrictions, the children stayed within a relatively short distance of their parents.

The scenario was repeated, but this time a clear physical boundary was erected around the outside of the picnic area. Again the children were encouraged to play wherever they wanted to. This time, the children wandered much farther, exploring the now-defined play area to its extremities.

What can we learn from this? Children enjoy more freedom when boundaries are clear; and children are more likely to feel safe, secure and happy when they know what they are allowed to do and when they are given clear rules. So, rather than limiting freedom, structure allows it.

Let's explore further some of the myths (as well as some alternative views) that impede parents from providing a helpful and appropriate level of structure in their children's lives.

Myth: It's too hard (or too much work).
Response: A little effort now means less effort (and greater rewards) later.

Developing a constructive framework for positive discipline requires effort, especially if you haven't done this before, but once you establish the foundations the benefits are immense and invaluable.

Myth: Structure will stifle my child's creativity.
Response: Structure provides freedom.

Just as art courses usually begin with either an exploration of colours and/or basic drawing, a sensible level of structure creates a solid base for growth; after all, how can you play successfully if you haven't learned the rules of the game?

Myth: It's healthy to have some spontaneity in life.
Response: Of course it is ... but a life without any structure is chaotic, and chaos is not healthy.

Myth: Imposing structure will just lead to conflict.
Response: Maybe, but only in the short term.

A classic example of short-term pain that leads to long-term gain is controlled crying for a baby: in the short term this process can be very distressing for all involved, but when used appropriately it can be effective and beneficial in the long term. The same principle applies to areas of family life in which structure is likely to prove advantageous.

Myth: There's no point trying to create structure because my partner won't back me up.
Response: Something's better than nothing.

Ideally, both parents should agree to participate in and apply these strategies equally, but if this is not possible then it's still worth trying. There is always the chance that your partner will enjoy the benefits of your efforts and want to become involved.

43. Short-term pain equals long-term gain

To raise happy children you will occasionally need to employ long-term strategies that aren't necessarily the easiest option. In fact, many of the recommendations in this book will be challenging to apply consistently, but building the right scaffolding – which includes clarifying priorities and developing effective, helpful habits – will definitely be worth it in the long run. I'm not saying it will be easy, but it will be worthwhile.

Try this simple exercise that allows you to work on a long-term strategy for your child's behaviour, without feeling overwhelmed. This should involve both parents. Pick one issue that concerns you, for example, your seven year old loses his possessions all the time. Think carefully about what a reasonable expectation of a child this age is, and, if in doubt, talk to your child's teacher. Most teachers would expect a seven year old to be able to keep track of their hat and put their lunchbox back in their bag. Let your child know clearly that this is what you expect. As he leaves for school each morning, remind him of this expectation. Set up a reward system, such as a gold star on a chart for every day he comes home with his hat and lunchbox. Don't forget to praise him when he does. When your child gets, say, twenty stars in row, give him a small but special treat – maybe he could have a sleepover or go on an outing. But remember, it is often not the treat itself that children love it is the fact they are being recognised for having achieved something significant.

Often by working on one simple problem at a time, your child's behaviour improves across the board. It can often feel like too much hard work for you, but from a long-term perspective it is much easier than having to constantly remind, coerce, or correct your child about ongoing problems – and much healthier for your mutual relationship.

44. Provide positive discipline and alternatives

When your child behaves in a way you are not happy with, it is worth trying a range of distraction strategies (depending on their age) before you consider discipline options. It is important to remember that children will make mistakes; you don't necessarily need to respond formally to every display of inappropriate behaviour. Instead, sometimes it's easier and more effective to try to diffuse the situation and move on.

There are several simple ways to achieve this, such as:

• change the topic of conversation
• direct your child to a new activity or task
• ask your child a question about something you know will interest them.

Most of us tend to deal with things badly when we're upset. Using distraction can reduce the intensity of distress, allowing your child to calm down enough to work constructively through the issue.

Vince and Angela have two very confident, smart and focused children: a ten-year-old girl and a seven-year-old boy. The flipside of these positive qualities is that both children are incredibly strong-willed and have been since they were very young. Vince and Angela used to argue, cajole and negotiate their way through every single issue with their kids – what they called the United Nations approach. But they came to realise that some issues needed to be dealt with quickly and efficiently, such as who owned which toy, what television program to watch and what clothes to wear. Now when they get the sense that an argument is brewing over a minor issue they use distraction. For example, the children were having a fight over a toy. Angela whipped the toy away, put it on a high shelf then suggested they go for a walk instead. Another time their ten year old was complaining while shopping because she couldn't buy a particular item of clothing that Angela thought was inappropriate. Angela suddenly remembered they had to choose a present for Nana's birthday, and she needed her daughter to help her. By looking after minor points of contention in this way Vince and Angela can spend more time having positive discussions with their kids on things such as books, outings, school and friends.

45. Discipline is not corporal punishment

I believe that discipline is essential for raising happy children, and that it can and should be a positive experience for children and parents. If conducted and delivered appropriately – there is absolutely no need for it to involve physical contact or pain – discipline provides a structure that is helpful and reassuring to all involved.

On page 74 I discussed the ways in which structure creates freedom, and order allows for creativity. Discipline is really no different – when applied appropriately it is an enormous positive.

I'd like to share this practical and constructive advice from Leora, a parent and subscriber to The Happiness Institute's e-newsletter. She emailed these thoughts in response to a call for positive parenting tips from our readers:

> *Identify when your kids are tired or not feeling 100 per cent – at these moments you're allowed to be a little inconsistent with your rules. As adults we know when we feel tired and we adjust our activities accordingly. Kids can't articulate this. So when their behaviour is 'off', give them a cuddle; it's not the time to win the 'You can't watch TV' war.*
>
> *Boundaries and rules help create security, but being flexible and reading your children's signals adds to your children's sense of self and shows you understand them. Remember that kids have 'off' days too.*

46. Balance consistency with flexibility

One of the constant challenges for parents is finding a balance between consistency and flexibility. There is no easy solution to the problem of when to stick to your guns and when to bend a little, but as long as you understand the need for balance you'll probably hit the mark. As parents, we need to remember we won't get it right 100 per cent of the time!

How do we achieve consistency? If you are raising your child with your partner try to act as one. You might have slightly different parenting styles, which is fine, but your basic approach shouldn't differ in any significant way.

Another thing to keep in mind is that consistency does not mean you have to treat all your children the same. Each child is unique and will respond in their own way to different approaches (and punishments). Your responses need to be tailored to your child's gender, personality and needs. Explain to your children why you feel it is appropriate to offer them different responses, and remain consistent in your underlying principles and philosophy.

47. Positive reinforcement – what is it?

One of the most powerful ways to encourage your child to engage in a desirable behaviour is to use positive reinforcement. Positive reinforcement occurs when a particular behaviour is followed by a response (called a reinforcer) that is designed to increase the chances of the behaviour being repeated.

For example, let's imagine that every time a child raises their hand to answer a question in their classroom they are given ten cents. It wouldn't take long before every child is trying to answer more questions. In this instance, ten cents has become the reinforcer to encourage hand-raising – and effectively, the desire to answer questions.

Some parents and experts believe that rewarding children for good behaviour is not a good idea because it decreases their motivation to do something because they know it's the right thing to do rather than because they're going to receive a reward.

Rewards *can* have a negative influence on a child's motivation to perform a task if (a) the reward is not closely related in time to a specific behaviour and/or (b) the reward is not tangible. These problems can easily be avoided by not providing rewards for behaviours your child is already displaying well and by using clear and specific criteria for reinforcement. Overall, when used appropriately, rewards do not have a negative or harmful influence on a child's motivation to perform a task.

Two of the most powerful reinforcers for children are praise and attention. Never underestimate the power of a simple 'Well done'. So, praise your child when they are engaging in helpful, happy behaviours, and ignore them if they're doing things you consider to be undesirable. Using positive reinforcement to promote positive behaviours is far more effective than using punishment to reduce negative behaviours – put simply, you'll have far more success (and greater joy) if you focus on what's right more than if you focus on what's wrong. Read the following chapter to learn how to put positive reinforcement into action (see page 84).

'Don't give it any oxygen' is one of Paul's favourite parenting tips. He has three boys under five and has become an expert at knowing what to pay attention to and what to ignore. Because the boys are so close in age parental attention is a prized commodity. Paul has found that paying attention to good behaviour – noticing when one of the boys finishes all his dinner, puts on his shoes by himself or packs away his toys – is a very effective way of ensuring that the desirable behaviour continues. By contrast, ignoring a child who is being overly sooky or bossy seems to be all the punishment that's required in most situations, although Paul always intervenes when one of the boys becomes verbally or physically aggressive.

48. Positive reinforcement – how to do it

Given the incredible potential and power of using positive reinforcement to play, grow and build happiness (see page 82), I think it's worth providing a brief summary of the key points:

- The reward needs to be something that is clearly positive for the receiver, not necessarily for the giver. For example, my daughter is not a big fan of ice-cream. Once, some time ago, when I offered to take her for an ice-cream as a reward for something she'd done the offer was rejected!

- The reward should be delivered as close as possible (in terms of time) to the desired behaviour that is being acknowledged. As any parent knows, something that happened a few hours ago, one hour ago, sometimes even ten minutes ago is ancient history to children. The power of the reinforcement is significantly reduced the longer you delay the reward.

- Ensure reinforcement is obvious. Make it clear that you're doing what you're doing because your child performed the specific behaviour or action.

- Reinforcement should initially be delivered as often and as consistently as possible; over time, the frequency should be gradually reduced, and eventually faded out (although praise should be continued indefinitely, as often as possible). Eventually, your child will learn that the behaviour is worth doing simply because it's right or good.

49. Accept that change takes time

If you want to change aspects of your child's behaviour you need to accept that it will take time – after all, few people manage to change overnight; we all need some in-between time to develop new habits.

For example, most children find catching a ball a bit difficult at first, which leaves a parent or coach two options: they can wait until the child can catch the ball properly and then congratulate them, or they can reward the child's attempts as they learn how to catch the ball. Clearly the latter approach is more motivating and effective in achieving the desired outcome sooner.

The trick to this approach is to gradually raise the bar: the child could be rewarded firstly for holding out their hands; then when they hold out their hands and touch the ball; then when they catch the ball sometimes; and then finally, when they're catching the ball on most occasions.

Maybe you could consider using a star chart to encourage your child to achieve their goals. This simple but powerful method incorporates all the principles of positive reinforcement.

50. Spend quality time with your child

Living in the present is an important happiness strategy, as long as your aim is not to escape life but to fully experience it.

I know how easy it is to get distracted when you're at home with the kids. It feels like there are hundreds of other things you could or should be doing instead of just playing with them. Of course you need time to yourself, but remember that one of the most important aspects of raising happy children is spending time with them – and when you do, really *being* with them.

What does this mean? It means focusing on them and their needs, doing what they want to do and not necessarily what's easiest or most convenient for you. It means getting down to their level and into their head space and fully engaging with them and their energy.

Try the following approaches when you spend time with your child:

- Turn off the TV and leave your phone out of sight and ear-shot.
- Forget about what you think you need to do later and just focus on what you're doing with your child now.
- When you notice yourself feeling rushed, stressed or confused, pause for a moment and take three slow, deep breaths. This can often be enough to calm you down so that you can return to the present and focus on your child.
- If your child seems especially needy for your attention stop what you're doing and spend at least five special minutes with them doing something they enjoy.
- Whenever you get the opportunity, take a few minutes for yourself to just 'be', to forget your worries and responsibilities.

- Take five minutes first thing in the morning to think about what you have to do, and imagine positive outcomes for each activity or task. In a similar way, take five minutes at the end of the day to review the day and identify what went well.

Nick works a seventy-hour week running his own business, which means his wife looks after things at home. Things were working out well until it become apparent that their oldest child, nine-year-old Carl, was starting to complain that he never had enough 'dad time' and that the dads of his school friends did more with their kids. Because of the amount of time he spent away from the house, Nick had all sorts of chores to do on the weekend. Rather than stop these altogether, Nick started to involve Carl in his activities. He was careful to make these activities fun and engaging and not just hard work. A highlight was the construction of a new set of shelves for the kids' room. Carl went with his dad to the hardware store, chose the wood, then helped his dad construct and varnish the shelves. Nick and his wife also made a rule that half a day each weekend would be set aside for a fun activity or outing, such as a family movie, a trip to the beach, a bushwalk or some sort of game.

51. Teach your child the benefits of mindfulness

Practising to be a mindful parent (see page 35) will help you reduce and manage the stressful moments, more fully enjoy the positive moments, and ultimately be a more effective parent.

When you feel like you have mastered the concept of mindfulness, also known as being in the moment or enjoying the moment, show your child how they can benefit from being mindful too. Start off with simple things they'll understand, and as they develop so will the skills needed to fully appreciate being mindful:

- Mindful eating: encourage your child to focus on the taste and texture of their food rather than watching TV, reading or playing during mealtimes.
- Mindful walking: encourage your child to be mindful of the physical movements and the sounds and sights around them as they walk.
- Mindful breathing: encourage your child to just sit, for at least a minute, and be mindful of their breath coming in and out of their body.

52. Understand and practise unconditional positive regard

Unconditional positive regard is a term mostly used by therapists who believe that showing their client unconditional positive acceptance and withholding judgement provide the best conditions for the client to achieve personal growth, because all people have the internal resources, strengths and abilities required to solve their own dilemmas and to achieve their best.

As a therapist, coach and parent I think this useful clinical tool can also be a very useful parenting tool; and you don't need to be a trained therapist for it to work! Instead, simply:

- accept your child for who and what they are
- believe that by doing so you're increasing the chances of them being the best they can be
- look for evidence that your child has all the resources they need to be happy and successful
- listen without making assumptions and without pre-judging.

53. Love as much as you can, then more

How do you let your child know that you love them? Hidden love is not much use to anyone. Love needs to be seen, felt, heard, touched and lived. Love needs to be overt, and not always subtle. Love, especially for children, should be celebrated loudly, often and in all manner of circumstances.

In my experience many parents don't show their love enough for several reasons, including:

- a fear of 'spoiling' their children (this is especially true for boys)
- a belief that too much of a good thing is not a good idea
- uncertainty about what to do because their parents didn't know what to do and couldn't act as positive role models.

In recent times overt displays of emotion have become unpopular; while I'm all for managing and controlling emotions (especially inappropriate ones), I can't see any reason why we should hide our love, happiness, joy and passion.

When it comes to raising happy children, there's no doubt that children brought up in a loving, positive environment will benefit from their observations of, and experiences with, these emotions. More than likely, they'll go on to be happier people and ultimately happier and better parents when it's their turn.

54. Integrate the 'Losada Ratio'

To develop and enhance positive relationships, the ratio of positive to negative interactions should be at least five (positives) to one (negative) in our personal relationships and three to one in our relationships in the workplace. This is referred to as the 'Losada Ratio' due to the intensive relationship work done by psychologist Dr Marcial Losada.

The unfortunate reality, however, is that most people in most relationships get nowhere near that! One of the most powerful ways we can improve our chances of raising happy children is to increase the ratio of positive to negative interactions with them.

Inherent in this is the premise that happiness is not a selfish pursuit but is focused on caring for and taking an interest in other people. It makes sense that people who are generous, altruistic, loving and compassionate are happier than those who are not.

When you are with your child, consciously work on increasing the proportion of positive (compared to negative) comments you make. This does not mean ignoring problems, but focusing on them in a positive, constructive way.

55. Aim for quantity time as well as quality time

In recent years the phrase 'quality time' has become increasingly popular, and although I recognise that quality time is important (see page 86), we must not overlook the fact that we significantly increase our chances of having quality time with our children (or with anyone else for that matter) if we spend lots of time with them.

Quality time should not just be about taking your child for ice-cream, to the movies or shopping for a new toy. These activities are great but so too are the spontaneous moments and comments during dinnertime, while they're playing in the bath, the accidents that occur while you're washing the car together, the chat you have when you're walking to school, or the amazing insights revealed while simply drawing on some paper with crayons.

Most children love nothing more than spending time with their parents, and most parents feel the same way about spending time with their children, so everyone wins.

56. Talk to your child

If we can to talk to our kids effectively, and in turn they can talk to us effectively, we all stand a better chance of them being able to stand up for what they believe in and resist being led astray.

Help your child identify their thoughts before, during and after interactions, especially difficult or challenging ones. Help them recognise unhelpful thoughts such as 'No one will like me if —' or 'If I don't do what they're doing I'll —', and also to challenge these thoughts and replace them with more helpful, realistic and positive ones (see page 43).

Teach your child to stand by their opinions, beliefs and values, and to respect the fact that many people they come across in life will have different opinions, beliefs and values – and that's okay.

The best communication occurs when all parties are able to remain calm. This is not to say we shouldn't experience or express emotion, but it is difficult to manage your thoughts, listen to others and be appropriately assertive if you're highly charged, emotional or distressed.

> *Pam has a very bright six-year-old daughter, Claire. One day Claire asked her mum why she said thank you for doing the things she was meant to do, such as cleaning her room. As Claire pointed out, no one said thanks to Pam for going to work or putting on the washing. Pam and Claire talked about this for a while, and decided that what Pam should say were things like 'Well done' and 'Tidying your room is very helpful'.*

57. Listen to your child

As many before me have said, there must be a reason why we have two ears and only one mouth! One way to show your child you love them is to really listen to them. For many decades psychologists have recognised the importance of an approach often referred to as 'active listening', believing that listening is not just a passive activity during which you sit back and hear what someone has to say.

Active listening involves the following:

- Stop anything else you're doing and look at the person speaking to you.
- Listen not just to the words but also to the emotions and meaning behind the words.
- Take an interest in what the other person is talking about.
- If you are unclear about what they're trying to say, restate what the person said (for example, 'Am I right in thinking that what you're saying is —?')
- Ask questions and don't be afraid to acknowledge if your attention drifted or if you didn't fully comprehend something.
- Be aware of your own feelings and opinions and how these might be affecting your interpretation of what you are hearing.
- If you have to state your views do so only after you have listened.

58. Be a family – eat, play and hang out together

This idea is, in some ways, an extension of the theme of quantity time (see page 92) as opposed to quality time (see page 86). It is also more than that – in the way that a sports team is more than the sum of its parts, in the way that a marriage is more than two individuals, and in the way that a family is more than just parents and children.

A happy family, quite simply, is made up of people who respect each other's privacy, individuality, strengths and differences but also engage in activities together as one. As a result, a happy family will disagree at times but will also enjoy the wonders of collaboration and interaction.

Being a family involves engaging in special events and activities as well as mundane, day-to-day tasks. Consider some of these activities you can do as a family:

- preparing, cooking and eating meals
- washing up, cleaning the house, washing the car
- going for walks
- going on outings and adventures
- learning about new things
- writing stories and/or making home movies
- watching and playing sport
- making up plays, songs and artworks
- playing games.

59. Remember to have fun

Playing and having fun can take many forms. In addition to all the formal games and sports with which you're no doubt familiar, consider some of the examples listed below that can be used to enhance the mood at dinnertime, on a long drive or while walking:

- The Question Game is one of our kids' favourites and simply involves asking your children age- and interest-appropriate questions for them to try to answer (note: this is about having fun, not about competing).
- Making up stories is great fun – incorporate characters that resemble family members, or events that have recently occurred in your life.
- Asking the question, 'What's the best thing that happened to you yesterday, last week, last year?', is a great way of getting kids engaged in fun, imaginative chatter.

One of the great side benefits of teaching or encouraging your child to have fun is that it helps foster a sense of humour. A sense of humour is one of our greatest protections against depression and one of the best guarantees of being able to rise above difficult situations. Abraham Lincoln was one of history's most famous sufferers of depression but also a man with a seriously well-developed sense of humour. He said he laughed so that he did not weep and used humour to 'whistle off sadness'. Most kids can be cajoled out of a bad mood with a funny anecdote or a bit of horseplay. A child with a good sense of humour will learn to see the world as a warmer, more welcoming place and will start to learn how to negotiate their way around some of the more absurd kinds of behaviour and situations that are an inevitable part of daily life.

Happiness is much more likely to come to those who 'do' rather than to those who 'buy', so teach your kids the value of engaging in all of life's experiences and enjoying and appreciating the essence of life, rather than focusing on the attainment of material possessions.

Amy's parents divorced when she was two. Her mum never remarried, but her dad married four times. As she grew up she had a range of stepmums, an unofficial stepdad and an assortment of siblings. The comment she hears most about her unusual family is, 'You're surprisingly normal, considering.' But Amy is always quick to point out that she believes it is because of her family, not despite them, that she has turned out so well. Her parents were gifted in the art of self-deprecating humour. Rather than try to validate their decisions they explained them as part of the rich fabric of life. They always made sure Amy felt secure in their love. Family life, with both parents, was sometimes unpredictable and a bit chaotic but always warm, loving and full of fun. Most importantly, neither parent ever criticised one another in front of Amy. She grew up understanding that her parents, particularly her dad, had not quite mastered the finer points of marriage, but both were essentially good people who cared a great deal for their daughter.

60. Let your child be a child

During the course of writing this book I came across the story of little Johnny who arrived home one day with an ice-cream cone in each hand. His mother asked, 'Did you spend all your pocket money?'

'Nope,' he said, 'I didn't spend any.'

'Did someone buy the ice-cream cones for you?' she asked.

Johnny shook his head and seeing a worried look come over his mother's face added, 'And don't worry, I didn't steal them.'

'Then where did they come from?' she asked.

'I put a chocolate cone in one hand and a vanilla cone in the other, then I told the shop assistant she could get the money from my pocket as long as she was careful of Frankie, my pet spider.'

I'm not advocating theft or deceit, but I can't help wonder whether there are times when we overlook or underappreciate the ingenuity of our children and instead label creativity and play as naughtiness.

Children need to have fun and play. Most children love to play, but sometimes parents can inadvertently discourage this when they enforce the need to be serious. Making a game out of something mundane can help your child enjoy otherwise unpleasant tasks.

Marike is an Australian living in Thailand. She has a three-year-old daughter named Cate. Marike has learnt a lot about parenting from being around Thai families. She loves the way the children are an integral part of family life, and not just additions who must always vie for attention. She has tried to parent Cate in the same way. Whenever friends visit from overseas they often comment on the fact that Cate never seems to cry or complain or get bored and how easily she gets on with everyone, adults and children alike. Because she is so much a part of her parents' life and daily routines her play mimics their activities. Cate has loads of toys, given to her by well-meaning friends and relatives, but she is happiest when she is 'cooking' outside with a few broken cups, and leaves and berries or playing 'night bazaar', where she copies her dad opening his shop in the markets.

Section Four

20 ways to make learning safe and fun

This section focuses on all kinds of learning, not just the kind that happens at school. From the moment children are born they start to learn. What they learn is important, but it's how they learn that counts most. If learning is fun, safe and appropriate to an individual child's level of development, interests and temperament then the experience will be one they want to continue throughout their life. Parents can feel out of control when it comes to school learning; however, they can have a big effect on how children learn by fostering the right values and creating a supportive environment at home and by developing constructive and positive relationships with those in their child's learning community.

61. Foster a love of learning

It shouldn't surprise you to hear that children learn and perform better academically if they're happy. We've known for decades that in a 'training' context people learn better if they're having fun because when they're enjoying themselves they tend to be more energised, engaged and focused, so the goal when it comes to learning and education should be about having fun. This is especially relevant in the earlier years prior to secondary school, although ideally nothing much would change after that!

How can you help your child foster a love of learning?

- Focus on areas in which your child already has some interest. For example, if your child loves dinosaurs use them as the topic of study. There is no shortage of wonderful educational books that make learning about dinosaurs fun.
- Encourage your child to read, read, read! Whatever your child is interested in – sport, magic, art – good bookstores and libraries provide plenty of choice. The idea should really be that, within limits, it doesn't really matter what your child is reading or learning about in the early years as long as they're reading and learning.
- Ask your child's teacher to recommend reputable websites that involve educational and fun activities appropriate to your child's age. I've noticed in recent years the development of a number of wonderful websites and Internet games that make learning fun.

62. Foster a love of schooling

As I discussed in the previous entry (see opposite), children who are happy at school will more than likely perform well.

Most children go through stages of not liking school. It could be because of their teacher, or issues with peers such as bullying or not fitting in. If this happens to your child there are things you can do to help, including the following:

- Get involved in your child's school life: talk to them about their day, attend school functions, plays and events, and help out on tuckshop duties.
- Without overwhelming them, get your kids involved in extracurricular activities that will allow them to utilise their strengths and talents.
- Find ways to make school fun by creating projects at home that will help your child see how enjoyable learning can be.
- Ensure your kids are developing good relationships at school. For some this will come easily but for others it might require some additional attention. If your child has good friends at school they will enjoy being there.
- Try to identify problems early, and take action as soon as possible.

63. Set ground rules for homework

If we can teach our children to enjoy learning, exploring, investigating, reading and discovering the task of getting them to do the hard yards when it comes to homework will be far easier.

Remember, homework won't always be fun but it doesn't have to end in tears. Consider the following points when setting ground rules for your child:

- Make a special homework space that is clean and clear.
- Make a special homework time (routine is very helpful).
- Ask your child to complete their homework before playing (play and fun then become the reinforcer).
- Reinforce and reward good homework behaviour.
- Help out as much as you can and/or need to (attention is a potent reinforcer), but don't do it all for them.
- Keep a positive attitude about homework, and be supportive and encouraging.
- For older children who need to spend more time doing homework, encourage them to take regular short breaks.
- Allow your child input into all of the above.

64. Make homework fun

I believe young children shouldn't do too much homework – they should be allowed to play, have fun, relax and exercise – but obviously as they move through primary school and beyond they will be assigned more and more homework. Why not consider the following options to make this fun:

- Make a game out of it.
- Provide rewards if homework is completed in a certain way or by a certain time.
- Tie the homework in to your child's interests and passions. For example, maths can easily be worked into sporting scores, and science can be incorporated into cooking and gardening.

Harry, aged eight, always complained that his maths homework was too hard. His dad Bill had to sit with him and work through it question by question, every week. One day when the family was playing Monopoly it became quite clear that Harry was able to do many of the calculations in his head very quickly. From then on, Bill stopped sitting with Harry while he worked figuring that Harry was relying on him rather than making the effort his son was clearly capable of. Instead, Bill devised ways to make Harry's homework a game. He would time Harry using a stopwatch, make a big show of marking all the questions, and pretended to be a game show host, asking Harry lots of questions about his work. Harry gradually focused more and complained less. He came to understand that while his dad would support him he wasn't going to do his homework for him.

65. Learn outside of school

There's no doubt that a love of learning is closely associated with happiness, and that learning can (and probably should) take place not just at school but at home – and everywhere else, for that matter!

If your child enjoys learning outside of school they'll more than likely enjoy learning at school too. And remember, learning is much more than simply accumulating knowledge.

Consider some of these suggestions:

- Find out whatever it is your child is interested in and find ways for them to learn as much about it as possible.
- Make their interests your interests – this will help them learn as well as strengthen your relationship.
- Attend great learning environments such as museums, where interaction is encouraged and learning is fun.
- Keep your child busy when they're young – if their time is spent doing educational activities it's a win–win situation.
- Learning outside of school is a great way to enable your child to fully utilise their strengths and develop their talents. If they enjoy music at school, why not arrange extra lessons in a specific instrument? If they like bike riding, get them into a BMX club.
- Be conscious of overdoing it; remember that your child needs time just to be, play, rest and relax.

66. Encourage curiosity

Every parent at some stage has tired of their child asking, 'Why?'. At times, when these 'Why?' questions seem to come thicker and faster than a celebrity controversy, it's easy (and understandable) to just say, 'Because!' or to shut down the conversation as quickly as possible. (I know because I've fallen into this trap.) As tempting as this response is, we should try to avoid it; instead, we should encourage our kids to ask why.

Why? Because curiosity is closely related to happiness. Curiosity is also closely aligned with a love of learning, which ultimately is what will help our children become good students and successful in life.

Learning shouldn't be just about the accumulation of facts and knowledge, but about understanding what's behind the knowledge and how to interpret information (including how to tell good information from bad).

How do we achieve this? By asking 'Why?'.

Developing curiosity is also a great lesson in patience for parents, and if you look at it positively you might also learn something. If you don't know the answer to a question your child asks look it up together – the learning experience can become a bonding experience.

67. Focus on established areas of interest

Consider the following scenario, which was a small part of a large research study conducted in many different countries.

Participants were asked to consider how they would respond if their child came home with the following grades:

- As in English and Social Studies
- C in Biology
- F in Maths.

Most parents focused on the F in Maths, responding with something along the lines of: 'We need to focus on the maths. My kid's failing in this subject and we need to help him out.'

You might be reading this thinking, 'That's not me! I'd focus on the As.' If this is really the case then well done, but do you do this in all domains of your life or the lives of your children?

Alternatively, you might be reading this thinking that it's perfectly reasonable to focus on the F. You're at least partly right. But reasonable is not always best, and focusing on positives is far more effective and powerful than focusing on negatives, so the best approach would be to concentrate on the As.

Whether it's in the workplace, at school or at home, praise for positive performance is associated with more than 70 per cent improvement. This contrasts with constructive criticism, which is something that you might do for the C, which leads to just 20 per cent improvement. And finally, ignoring or doing nothing has negligible effect.

I'm not suggesting you ignore failures or areas in which you or your child could improve; I am, however, advocating a slight rethink that involves reconsidering the extent to which you attend to Fs in comparison to the As. Sure, focus on areas that need improvement, but make sure you also devote time to reviewing and reinforcing the As.

Gina was in despair when she went to the first parent–teacher night at her daughter's high school. One teacher after another told her that her daughter Maggie was struggling with her schoolwork. The only teacher who had positive comments was the music teacher, but she was rushed and didn't have time to discuss things in detail. At home Maggie had been telling Gina that she didn't like high school and wanted to go back to her old primary school. Maggie had always been a good singer so Gina encouraged her to audition for the music ensemble at school in the hope this would give her something positive to focus on. Maggie was very self-conscious, but with the help of their neighbour's son, who already played guitar in the ensemble, she decided to go ahead with the audition. Her audition went so well she not only got a place, but the ensemble leader rang Gina personally to comment on the quality of Maggie's voice. On the basis of this, Gina decided to pay for private singing lessons for Maggie. Over the months, Maggie's singing got better and better. She started to love going to ensemble rehearsals, and gradually came to feel very comfortable about being at high school. This increased confidence flowed over into her school work. She still struggled, but she engaged more and took responsibility for asking when she needed help.

68. Don't focus on obstacles

One morning my son and I shared an hour in a park where some old donated toys had been left lying around for kids to enjoy. He started playing with a plastic truck, and as he prepared to move it along the imaginary path he had created it became apparent the other toys were in his way.

As a rational adult my first reaction would have been to pick up the toys that were in the way so I could move the truck along what I'd thought to be the ideal path. But, as far as I could tell, my son didn't consider this option – instead, he simply picked up the truck, carried it over the toys and continued along his merry way.

It got me thinking about what we do (or don't do) when things get in the way of our happiness. Do you focus too much on obstacles and what you need to do to remove them? Do you allow roadblocks to distract your attention from the ultimate goal (such as happiness or success)?

What would happen if, like my son, we simply stayed focused on the end goal and what we wanted to achieve despite the challenges that got in the way?

69. Take responsibility when dealing with members of the school community

Sometimes parents can overreact or react very emotionally to issues to do with their child's schooling. Sometimes this is because we are not entirely sure what our responsibilities are and either overreach or remove ourselves entirely from the equation. For many of us, powerful emotional buttons are pressed when we start taking our kids to school. Without quite realising it, we are reminded of our own school days. For many of us, school marked our first foray into a world without our parents. Alongside the fun and excitement were times of drama, anxiety, and sometimes humiliation. These memories can come flooding back at different points in our child's schooling making us feel more vulnerable than we would like.

These feelings express themselves in different ways. Some of us feel traumatised, others may feel the need to control, and others become defensive and critical. Here are some examples of instances of parental overreaction:

- When Christine took her first child to her first day at school, she found it hard to leave. When the teacher gently suggested she go, Christine started crying. Her child was very unnerved. 'Why is Mum leaving me in this place she feels so unhappy about?', the five year old wondered.
- Michael was very concerned about his son's grades. He went to see the Grade 3 teacher, who said Michael's child was a solid but average performer. Michael got angry at this point, saying that

he knew his child was a high achiever and the teacher wasn't doing enough to encourage him.

- Lily is an actress. Her child Anna is comfortable on stage but not overly enthusiastic. When Anna was overlooked for the school play Lily went to see the principal to complain.

- Eight-year-old Sal had a fight with her best friend, Mia. Sal's mum came home after a hard day at the office. When she heard about the fight she got angry and rang Mia's mum to tell her that she thought Mia was bullying her daughter.

These things happen to people who would normally think of themselves as fairly calm, responsible human beings. Sometimes, when it comes to our kids, our sense of proportion and responsibility disappears, creating problems for ourselves and our kids that can reverberate for months, if not years.

When in such a situation, take pause and remind yourself that you are the adult not the chid. Make a point of taking responsibility for yourself and your emotions when talking to a teacher, other parents and other people's children. A friend of mine who is quite involved in her children's primary school says she always treats people in her school community as if they were her work colleagues (in other words, with a HR policy at the forefront of her mind). Perhaps the easiest and most rewarding way of feeling in touch or in control of what is happening at school, and with your kids' friends, is to get involved: join the parents' committee; have coffee with other parents; make a point of helping out in the classroom. This will give you a sense of investment in your child's school and the motivation for wanting to help create a positive environment for all to enjoy. You will find yourself much better placed to respond to situations as they arise rather than react.

70. Know when your child needs a break from learning

As much as I believe learning is important, there are simply times to learn and times not to learn.

In recent years we've seen a trend towards over-parenting, hyper-parenting and downright bad parenting. Many parents, concerned about their child's ability to get ahead in an increasingly competitive world, believe that every second of every day must be utilised to help their child stay ahead of the pack.

This is, quite simply, overkill. We all – adults and kids – need rest from thinking and being active. Have you ever come up with a great idea when you weren't even trying? It's often when we're not actively learning that we are able to be the most creative.

By all means encourage your child to learn but also allow them time to not learn and to just be!

Nina had to write a speech for English as part of a Grade 12 assignment. She didn't like English and didn't feel she did well at the subject, so it was a big deal. She stayed at her desk for four hours, but it just wasn't happening. Her mum suggested she do something else for a while, something completely different. Nina decided to watch one of her favourite movies on DVD. When it was over, she went back to her desk and wrote the speech in two hours flat. She ended up getting an A for it. She learnt a big lesson about the need to sometimes relax and focus on something entirely different from the task at hand.

71. Teach your child to keep going

Perseverence is a very important part of learning (see page 66). Teaching your child perseverance – how to push on when things aren't going their way or when a goal is worth pursuing – will serve them well all their lives. (Of course there comes a time when stopping a pursuit is the best option – I discuss this in the following chapter, on page 116.)

Encourage your child to see the benefits of persevering with something even if they don't show great skills at the outset; if they show an interest that's enough to warrant spending some time on the task.

One of the toughest things for a parent is watching a child with potential 'throw in the towel'. Here are some tips for when you think they could be heading down that path:

- How long have they been doing the activity? Have they given it a go? If not, suggest a time in the future when they can stop if they still don't enjoy it.
- Ask them why they're not enjoying it. Can these problems be fixed? They may not want to tell you the real reason. Calmly listen to what they say, and use Socratic questioning (see page 42) to help them come up with a solution.
- Ask them to list the positives and negatives of quitting or continuing, and then weigh up these options together.
- If they are adamant they want to stop ask if they would like to do something different instead. Try not to be pushy.
- Reinforce the concept of working hard to achieve your goals. Remind them of others (famous people, relatives, school friends) who have worked hard at something they love and achieved happiness from the result.

- Ask yourself why you want your child to continue this pursuit. Is it to make you happy? Or is it really for them? Make sure the benefits are for them and not for you.

Elizabeth and Zara are twelve-year-old twins with very different personalities. Elizabeth is quick to learn and very easily bored. Zara learns more slowly but tends to stick with and eventually master difficult tasks. When it comes to perseverance, the girls' parents have upheld Zara as the model letting Elizabeth know she is too flighty and too impatient by comparison. But this opinion was challenged by the girls' Grade 6 teacher at the half-yearly parent–teacher meeting. She pointed out that Elizabeth had an excellent big-picture approach to learning, a well-developed sense of curiosity, and an ability to get the overall gist of a subject very quickly. As a result of this conversation, the parents adopted a different approach with Elizabeth. As an example, Elizabeth had complained of being bored with her piano lessons. Rather than insist she continue or allow her give up, her parents found a teacher with an approach that suited Elizabeth's learning style. Instead of working on difficult classical pieces, Elizabeth now plays a lot of pop and rock; most recently she worked her way through the entire Beatles' repertoire, often managing to learn a song in a single session before moving on.

72. Know when enough is enough

I was recently reminded why Australia has an emu and a kangaroo on our coat of arms: supposedly it's because neither of these animals can walk backwards.

Not taking a backwards step is typically seen as a positive thing, and in many instances I've no doubt it is, but we also need to be clear about the difference between positive perseverance and plain stubbornness – there are times when 'giving up' should really be considered an appropriate retreat.

The way we interpret what we and others do significantly impacts how we feel, including our motivation. Surely there are times when we need to recognise we've headed too far in the wrong direction; it's then time to cut our losses, face our embarrassment (if needed) and move on (preferably in a different direction). After all, head and brick wall can only meet so many times before it's detrimental.

73. Learn to resist peer pressure

Peer pressure is an unfortunate fact of life; we've all heard stories about the lengths some children will go to in order to feel accepted. It can affect all areas of your child's life, from their choice of clothes and music to how they behave at school.

A strong foundation of values and priorities will help you equip your child with skills to cope with this pressure. Teach them to differentiate between right and wrong. Develop effective communication strategies, which might involve learning how to say 'no' – but remember that this is much easier said than done. There's no doubt there are situations where saying 'no' will lead to your child being pressured or bullied.

With this in mind, it might be useful to arm your child with some distraction strategies, delaying tactics or even excuses that will help them find their way out of situations without overtly saying 'no'. One of the best excuses is to simply blame the parents: 'My parents won't let me' is a powerful statement that every teenager understands. You can help your kids by assuring them you don't mind being characterised as overly strict if it helps get them out of tricky situations.

74. Learn to go with peer pressure

In the previous chapter (see page 117) I discussed the potential peer pressure has to cause significant problems for your child; now I want to focus on the elements of peer pressure that may actually help your child grow, develop and strive to be their best. In many ways, peer pressure is a normal phenomenon – we are, after all, social animals, and it's perfectly appropriate for children (and, for that matter, adults) to want to be part of a group and feel like we belong.

The term peer pressure is usually used in the context of someone feeling influenced to do something they wouldn't normally do or, alternatively, feeling influenced not to do something they would normally do, but I believe this is only part of the equation.

Another way of looking at peer pressure is as our way of fitting in, of being part of a community, and that's not such a bad thing. Within limits, it's okay if our children are succumbing to peer pressure. They need to fit in, forge strong relationships and identify with their peers in order to feel secure in these interesting teenage years.

My point is that peer pressure should not always be considered in a negative light; whether we like it or not it's a reality and we need to help our children work with it and find the balance between appropriately fitting in and being an individual.

We need to be realistic and accept that our children will, from time to time, do things they know aren't right because their friends are doing them and they didn't want to be left out or picked on. We should take a stand, however, if these behaviours are illegal, improper, unethical or in some way harm another person. It's a bit like choosing your battles and accepting you might lose a few fights in order to ultimately win the war.

Eight-year-old Raff is an only child. He has always been a very fussy eater. For example, there are times when he will only eat white food. Raff's best friend's family invited him to join them for a long weekend down the coast. Raff had never been away from his parents before so he was nervous. His mum warned the other parents about Raff's eating habits, but they didn't seem too phased – they had four kids of their own, so they had seen it all. At the first meal Raff hardly ate anything. His friend's mum encouraged him to eat what the others were eating but didn't insist. Raff watched the other kids eat – he noticed how none of them complained and all of them ate everything on the plate in front of them. He thought that maybe the food was quite good and he should try it. With each meal he ate more and more. At the end of the three days he was eating every-thing the other kids were eating and very much enjoying being part of the tribe.

75. Develop positive relationships with peers

One of the many misconceptions surrounding happiness is that it is a selfish endeavour, but this couldn't be further from the truth! Happy people are far from being selfish people; they are altruistic, generous, kind and loving.

Happiness is not about just one person, it's also very much about all the people with whom that person interacts. Accordingly, raising happy children involves teaching and encouraging the development and maintenance of positive relationships.

There's a children's book that wonderfully and succinctly presents a great message for kids: being a good friend and having good relationships involves being there for others and helping out when necessary. In *That's What Friends Are For*, by Florence Parry Heide and Sylvia Van Clief, a wounded elephant can't get to a meeting with his friend. A succession of animals provides a variety of titbits of advice, none of which is in any way practical for the elephant (for example, a bird suggests that if he has a sore foot he should simply fly!). Finally, however, a wise and sensible friend suggests that they could go and fetch the elephant's friend and bring her to him, so problem solved.

Implicit in this great story is the message that real friends support each other, and that this involves much more than just providing advice. Teaching your child the benefits of this kind of support will improve their chances of finding fulfilling friendships and happiness in life.

76. Deal with bullying

Bullying can be physical or verbal, and these days it's not just face to face – it's happening via the Internet and mobile phones. The first step to helping your child deal with bullying is to educate them about what bullying is and what's not acceptable.

Bullying can be ignored and bullies can be avoided, but if this isn't possible, or if you have identified bullying as a serious or persistent issue, you need to take action as soon as possible. The following steps will help you help your child deal with bullying:

- Encourage your child to talk to you, or someone else they trust, if they are concerned about being bullied or if they know anyone else who is being bullied.
- Explain that by not taking action to stop bullying the situation will probably only get worse and will encourage the bully to continue their behaviour.
- Help your child resolve the situation themselves. For example, rehearse what they can say to a bully and prepare for any expected comebacks or taunts.
- Show them that appropriate use of humour can help defuse some situations, but, at the same time, care needs to be taken not to antagonise the bully.
- If your child isn't able to resolve the situation themselves get involved and talk to the appropriate people at your child's school or within the group in which the bullying is occurring.

77. Help your child develop positive relationships with teachers

The child–teacher (and in fact the parent–teacher) relationship is very important, and as such it should receive the same time and effort given to developing other relationships in your child's life.

Communication is the key. It is important to teach your child that their relationship with their teacher can be positive, supportive and fun, but it is not the same as their relationships with their parents or friends.

Encourage your child to appreciate and respect their teachers – look for their strengths and value their knowledge, position and desire to teach. Does your child understand what their teacher's role involves? Understanding this will help your child appreciate all the various tasks their teachers are required to perform, the many responsibilities they have and the ways they can positively influence your child's present and future.

Your child will not always get a brilliant teacher. When this happens use it as an opportunity to teach your child how to negotiate a less-than-perfect situation. If the standards really slip, by all means take it up with your school, but don't complain about the teacher in front of your child – the messages are too confusing and potentially damaging.

78. What does failing really mean anyway?

If you fall down seven times and get up eight, does that mean you've failed? We don't consider our toddlers have failed when they first try to walk and fall over continuously; in fact we applaud their efforts. So why do we put so much emphasis on failure and why do we fear it so much?

Many happy and successful people consider that if they're not failing often they're not trying hard enough. This is a useful lesson for our children to learn: as long as they're learning from their mistakes and not repeating the same blunders over and over again, then the fall isn't so bad.

When teaching your child about failure, you first need to reframe – in your own mind – failure as an opportunity to learn, grow and improve; you can then more effectively communicate this to your child. You can do this in a number of ways, including celebrating 'failure' as a step towards success rather than punishing it. Tell your child about famous examples of failure that leads to success, such as Thomas Edison (if they like science), JK Rowling (if they like stories) and Don Bradman (if they like sport).

79. Overcome fears

It's normal for your child to experience a certain amount of anxiety, but when it begins to control their life, impact on normal function or stop them doing things they want to do it's neither normal nor helpful.

Here are some effective strategies that can help your child deal with anxiety:

- applied relaxation (see page 153)
- debating unhelpful negative thoughts with more helpful ones
- collecting evidence of successes and of situations that are incompatible with their fears
- slowly and gradually 'exposing' them to feared situations.

Helen's four-year-old son Jack is extremely shy. After a term at kindergarten he was not able to say hello to his teacher in the morning. Helen made a decision to focus on this single daily engagement in Jack's life in the hope that it would build up his confidence. During term holidays Helen told Jack that it was good manners to say hello and to look a person in the eye when doing so, and that this was what she expected of him. She knew he was capable of this, and was confident he could manage it. On the first day back, Jack was overwhelmed and could not manage a 'hello'. Helen took him outside for a pep talk, and when they walked back in Jack managed the greeting perfectly. Now he says it every day, complete with eye contact.

80. Act courageously

One of my favourite ways to encourage kids to act courageously is to get them to imagine what a courageous person would do in a situation, then pretend they're that person and behave accordingly!

There are times in life when we're all nervous – when we're looking over the edge of the bungee-jump platform, standing up in front of an audience or wondering if we should apply for that new job. Sometimes I think it's better to know than to not know, to regret the things we have done rather than the things we haven't done. So if you want your children to act with courage and determination, consider the following suggestions:

- Encourage your child to identify someone who's acted courageously, shown resilience or stood up for something they believe in. It could be one of their friends, a family member or even someone famous (a rock star, actor, famous historical figure or a character from a novel).
- Help them identify their courageous actions. What did these people actually do?
- How could your child apply something similar in their life?

Be careful when choosing superheroes as examples of people who act courageously. Jumping from tall buildings like Batman, scaling walls like Spiderman or trying to stop traffic like Superman are unrealistic courageous actions, particularly if you are dealing with young children.

Section Five

20 ways to ensure wellbeing

Your child's physical wellbeing directly affects their emotional wellbeing, their ability to perform at school, and the quality of the relationships they have with others. In recent years, we have heard alarming statistics about obesity rates and related lifestyle diseases. We know the way our children eat and exercise determines their physical (and emotional) health as adults. The good news is that solutions are not difficult, nor are they expensive. We can help our children become healthier by applying common sense and doing old-fashioned things like turning off the TV, eating a meal together, cutting out junk food, and sending them out to play. Other factors that will contribute to overall good health, covered in this section, include sleep, relaxation, and helping your child solve problems and avoid anxiety.

81. Be a good role model: identify and get rid of bad habits

The first two chapters of this section deal with you as a role model. How we eat, exercise, sleep, diet, relax and use substances such as drugs and alcohol – these are all family issues. Yes, there is the problem of excessive advertising and peer pressure, but the most important role model for your children, when it comes to their physical and emotional health, is you, the child's parent. Children don't question their parents' behaviour. A child who sees a parent drink a bottle of wine a night will think that's the way adults spend their evenings. A child who sees her mother constantly weighing herself will think such an obsession with weight is normal (see also pages 142–143).

We all engage in behaviours we're not happy about. In some cases these bad habits may simply be irritating or a nuisance, but in others they are destructive and self-defeating. So, why not stamp out these negative behaviours and replace them with more positive, productive actions?

General unhealthy and unhelpful habits include:

- smoking or drinking excessively
- eating poorly or too much
- spending too much time being inactive
- expressing road rage or other aggressive behaviours
- gambling excessively
- complaining constantly about a situation – work, a relationship – and not taking action to fix it.

Whatever your bad habits, the first step in changing them is to identify where you're going wrong and then commit to change. The best place to start is to monitor what you're currently doing, and when and where you most frequently do it. Although you might not always realise it, your behaviour is in many ways determined by the context or situation you're in.

Think about it: you don't always do exactly the same thing in response to certain stressors, do you? How you respond can be subtly affected by those watching you, your environment (whether you're at work or at home), how tired you are or how in control you feel.

Once you have identified negative habits, try the following plan:

- Determine what is motivating your behaviour. Is it a particular situation or environment (you smoke when you are at the pub) or an emotion (you stop eating when you feel nervous) that sets off the behaviour? There may be more than one situational or emotional factor that triggers the same behaviour – you smoke when at the pub, with friends and feeling nervous (emotional factor).
- Keep a diary note to remind yourself of how risky certain situations are. A good way of determining the risk is by thinking about how strong the urge is to revert to the bad habit.
- Weigh up the advantages and disadvantages of your current way of handling your feelings and difficult situations. What are the good and bad consequences attached to this behaviour? By determining the costs and benefits of your actions you can see what will motivate you to change your ways. What are you getting from it and what is it costing you?
- Remind yourself of the reasons for your decision to change.
- Write down an emergency plan for the most difficult situations and the strongest urges.

82. Be a good role model: build healthy habits

Once you've started to make some (even small) improvements and gains in getting rid of or cutting down on bad habits (see page 128) make sure you reward yourself with something meaningful and satisfying. In addition to reducing or ceasing bad habits, one of the best things you can do is build good healthy habits.

To work out which positive behaviours you want to start increasing you need to do some detective work. Start by thinking of someone you admire and work out what it is about them that you like. Then define specifically what it is they do that you'd also like to do. It could be, for example, that this person walks for half an hour, four mornings a week. Once you've worked this out, start to schedule and incorporate these activities and behaviours into your life, on a regular basis.

Making changes (even positive ones) isn't easy, so be prepared to make mistakes and know that you will forget your plan every now and then. Don't let slip-ups deter you. A setback is not a failure. In fact, it's best to label these occurrences as 'temporary setbacks' and to think of them as learning experiences because the more attempts you make at trying to change a behaviour, the more aware you will be of which situations are more difficult and when you're more likely to revert to your old ways.

Changing bad habits and building new ones can take a long time. The longer you give yourself to adjust and make life changes the more successful you are likely to be. Why not try some very simple things for starters:

- Determine just one thing you could do every day to improve yourself – one thing in an area you'd like to build healthy habits.

It could be to go for a short walk every morning, eat more fruit or drink more water, or practise applied relaxation or meditation for five minutes each day.

- Tell someone – ideally a supportive friend, colleague or family member – what you are planning to do, or if possible buddy up with someone for additional motivation.
- Reward yourself when you achieve your goal or even when you've taken a few steps in the right direction and moved a little closer to that goal.

83. Educate yourself and your child about healthy eating

In the past decade or so there has been a lot of talk about the obesity crisis and the best way to educate and re-educate families and children about the importance of good food. One theme that has emerged is that many families are losing basic but essential knowledge on how to shop for and prepare food. Many children can't identify what should be commonly used vegetables such as broccoli, and many adults don't know how to put together the simplest of meals. Jamie Oliver deals with this in his very popular TV series *Jamie's School Dinners* in England, while local food identity Stephanie Alexander has designed and implemented a comprehensive program for primary schools that teaches children how to grow and cook their own food.

The good news is that there is an enormous amount of information out there – cooking shows, magazines and books – for those of us who don't know much about cooking. Most of us know someone in our lives – a relative or friend – who is a good cook; go to that person and ask for a few lessons and some key tips for putting together family meals.

If you are already cooking up a storm, think of ways to involve your children. If children are intimately involved in the sourcing and preparation of food, it makes sense that they gain a good understanding of its nutritional benefits and come to savour the differences in flavour, texture and aroma.

Here are some tips on how to start your child on the road to a good food life:

- Look at recipe books together; talk about the different dishes your child might like to try.
- Take your child shopping for food. Try places other than supermarkets, such as small grocery stores and farmers' markets. Make a point of chatting to proprietors and encourage your child to ask questions about the different kinds of produce.
- Let your child help in the kitchen. Smaller children can do tasks such as weighing and adding ingredients; older children (from eight upwards), can do most tasks that adults can do – but it is important to teach them basic safety procedures when it comes to using knives, and getting things off the stove or out of the oven.
- Encourage your teenage child to cook independently. Discuss ideas for dishes and make sure there are healthy ingredients available for them to use.
- Eat together as a family at least four nights a week (see page 134).

84. Eat together as a family

The claims that have been made over the last decade or so about the benefits of eating together as a family are extraordinary. Various studies have found that the children of families that eat together regularly are:

- less likely to use drugs, alcohol and tobacco
- more likely to eat their vegetables – and have better nutrition generally
- less likely to suffer from depression later in life
- less likely to become anorexic
- more likely to do well at school.

This does not necessarily mean that eating together *causes* these outcomes, but there is certainly a strong correlation between eating together and a whole range of very positive behaviours and outcomes. Some researchers have gone as far as saying that making sure the family eats together most nights of the week is the single most important thing you can do as a parent. Eating together provides nourishment – families that eat together eat healthier food – and provides a sense of emotional connection, ritual and the opportunity to share information.

In families with adolescent children with lots of extracurricular activities and with two working parents, eating together can often seem like a logistical nightmare. However, most families find that by shuffling schedules, a family meal is possible at least three to four nights a week. Here are some tips for how to create the time and the right circumstances for a rewarding family meal:

- Decide how many family meals you can manage each week and on what nights, and stick to this plan.
- Make sure meals are served at a regular time.
- If your children complain because they are missing out on seeing friends, invite their friends to the family meal.
- Get your children involved in rituals such as setting the table and lighting candles.
- Get the conversation going with questions like: 'What was the best thing that happened today?' and 'What was the worst thing that happened today?'.
- Ask fun questions or have a family quiz where the focus is not so much on competition but on communicating and learning in a relaxed and enjoyable manner.
- Don't answer phones during the meal.
- Turn off the TV – research has found that having the TV on during meals negates most of the positive effects of eating together as a family.

85. Make healthy eating fun for young children

The best way to encourage your younger child to eat healthily is to make healthy eating a fun activity. The Raising Children Network's website, raisingchildren.net.au, has some simple, fun and tasty suggestions for healthy meals kids will enjoy. Try the following ideas to get your child involved in their healthy diet:

- Make faces or objects out of the food (mashed potato can be shaped into almost anything, and vegetables can also be cut up to represent pretty much anything including faces, animals, cars, spaceships or mermaids).
- Play games while eating: the 'I love' game involves taking turns telling each other what food you love most for breakfast, lunch and dinner; the 'gratitude' game involves contemplating how lucky we are to be eating what we're eating.

A colleague and friend of mine, Dr John Lang, who's completed some impressive work in this area, shared a great way to get kids to eat vegetables: allow them to write two lists, one with vegetables they don't want to eat and another with vegetables they're prepared to eat. These lists can be modified over time but the key is that the second list has to contain more items than the first list! To extend the game, have the child nominate one vegetable each week that they are willing to move from the first list to the second list.

86. Make healthy eating fun for older children

There is no reason why older children, from age eight upwards, should not be eating everything you are eating, with the exception of, say, a very hot curry. Children who regularly eat food that has a wonderful depth of flavour, interesting textures and enticing aromas will find themselves growing intolerant of fast food with its bland but overwhelming salty, fatty and sugary flavours.

Here are some ways to encourage your older child to be an adventurous eater:

- If the budget permits take the family out for dinner occasionally – try different cuisines, such as Indian, Chinese, Thai, Italian.
- If you buy an interesting product, such as a nice cheese, invite your child to taste it. Even if they don't like it ask them if they can explain why. Was it the flavour, the texture?
- Serve your child everything that you serve yourself. Your child will invariably tell you that they don't like this or that, but the fact that it is on their plate will mean that one day they'll try it and, who knows, maybe even like it.

Lindy was driving her two children interstate. They drove on large freeways and bypassed the local country towns. The meal options were limited to a selection of fast-food outlets that sat alongside the big service stations off the freeways. Ever since her children were small Lindy had fed them a healthy, varied diet. When they were younger they had asked for fast food, but that was mostly because of the giveaway toys that came with kids' meal deals. They had eaten fast food occasionally with other families but didn't enjoy it much. When Lindy suggested on their road trip that they pop into one of the fast-food outlets because there was nothing else available the children refused. Eventually they took a detour through one of the country towns and bought some sandwiches and fruit. Lindy still laughs at the thought of herself trying to talk her children into eating fast food.

87. Don't fuss with fussy eaters

Many families have fussy eaters. Very small children are often quite particular, which is understandable, but with some encouragement they often become more adventurous as they get older. Our job as parents is to keep offering children a healthy and varied diet. Three year olds don't know what's good for them – we need to teach them.

Many parents make the mistake of not re-offering certain types of food that have been left on the plate on previous occasions. Their child's dislike of, say, cucumbers becomes in their mind a permanent and invariable fact. But often it's just a matter of making sure the child is exposed to a particular foodstuff at different times. A friend of mine has a seven-year-old boy who would not eat green salad. One day, his mother decided she would put salad on his plate whenever she made it for the rest of the family. Sure enough, the little boy started eating salad and now loves it.

Food is an emotional issue – if you have any doubt, ponder the fact that our obsession with cookbooks is on par with our obsession with diet books. Parents can get very anxious when their children don't eat what's on their plate, and some parents end up catering to increasingly bizarre requests. Children are very good at working out what they can use in their favour, and many a child senses they can gain a little bit of power by fussing with their food. The trick in dealing with a fussy eater is to remain calm and consistent. Don't force them to eat unfamiliar food, but let them know you won't be making special meals. Children eat when they are hungry. If they miss a meal they are likely to make up for it later in the day or the next day.

A good trick for making sure children are eating what you want them to eat is to serve the very healthy parts of a meal first, when they are really hungry. If you are serving chops, mashed potatoes, carrots and beans, serve the carrots and beans first – and, to make it easier for yourself, offer them raw (although not to children under three).

As they get older many children start to express strong preferences, some of which are concerned with losing weight (see also page 142). Teenagers become vegetarians and vegans; some want low carbs, some want no carbs. If you are offering your family a balanced diet then the children should be able to organise themselves around this. As with younger children, avoid using food as a way of making teenagers feel special for expressing their very particular dietary preferences – it's a slippery slope. If, of course, your child does suffer from a genuine intolerance or allergy you'll need to get them properly diagnosed and make sure their diet is suitable.

88. Ensure your child eats healthily when away from home

This is a tough one because most of the time you won't be there to monitor what food your child buys or is served when you're not there. The key is to establish good eating habits at home and trust that your child's choices will be influenced by what you have taught them.

What children eat at school is very important. Many schools now have a healthy food policy for their canteens, and some promote a healthy lunchbox policy as well. Packing healthy lunchboxes every day is a big task for parents in busy families, but there are simple guidelines you can follow that will reduce the stress of having to decide what to add and what to leave out:

- make sandwiches with wholemeal or wholegrain bread
- pack lots of fruit
- pack cut-up raw vegies
- pack low-fat, low-salt savoury biscuits
- pack leftovers such as pasta, rice and noodles
- avoid most other processed foods, including flavoured yoghurts, muesli bars, juices and sweet biscuits
- provide a filled water bottle.

It is very important to promote the idea, especially among teenage girls, that just because someone else isn't eating doesn't mean they shouldn't. Teach your child to choose the healthiest option available and eat until they are just full. Be sure to read the chapters on pages 142–143 about helping your child develop a healthy body image.

89. Develop a family policy on weight and weight loss

Excluding extremes at either end of the spectrum (significantly over-weight or underweight), it's important for children (and, in fact, for all of us) to understand that we all come in different shapes and sizes.

It is very difficult to help children develop a positive mental atti-tude towards body size if you (or your partner) are constantly dieting. It is natural to want to be as fit and healthy as possible, but constant discussion about weight, accompanied by other evidence of obsessive dieting, will create a charged atmosphere around the issue of food and food intake. Using the scales all the time, denying yourself food and complaining a lot about weight gain are tricky messages for children to receive, particularly teenagers. If you do need to lose weight, advertise it to the family as a desire to get fit and stay healthy. Make a point of talk-ing to children in a positive way about their bodies and weight gain/loss, steering the discussion in the following ways:

- Help your child understand 'normal' and 'healthy' weight ranges, especially during adolescence.
- Help them critically assess and analyse media images and messages, including the 'abnormality' of many supermodels, movie stars and elite athletes.
- Guide them towards a goal of health rather than body size or weight.

90. Teach your child to accept their appearance

Variety is the spice of life! We all come in many shapes and sizes, and many things about our appearance can't be changed (without enormous risk and significant cost).

To explore this issue, try this activity: help your child think of famous people, such as actors, sportspeople and entrepreneurs, who might look a little unusual but who've found happiness, success and satisfaction. Discuss these identities and their success, despite their unique looks, with your child.

Ensure that you continually encourage your child to focus on what they can change (not on what they can't) and their strengths (not their perceived weaknesses).

Melinda's favourite Grade 7 assignment was for her Personal Development class. The teacher asked the class to find pictures of celebrities and photos of family and friends and to arrange these side by side on a large sheet of cardboard. The class then had to write about the differences between the two groups of people. Melinda noticed how warm and engaged the people in the personal photos looked and, by contrast, how fake and strained some of the celebrities looked. Although the celebrities were extremely well groomed and often very beautiful they didn't invite you into their world, nor did they look like the sort of people you wanted to spend time with. Melinda now finds she rarely, if ever, feels like imitating celebrities in her dress and behaviour.

91. Reduce screen time

There has been a lot of research lately into the amount of time children spend in front of a screen and the way this affects behaviour. One of the interesting findings is the link between excessive screen time and weight gain. When children cut down on the amount of TV they watch they lose weight. This is not because they necessarily increase their physical activity, but because they stop the steady snacking that is often associated with TV watching.

But this is not the only reason why you should encourage your child to reduce their screen time. For every minute they are in front of a screen they are not doing the following: engaging with you, engaging with their siblings, reading, doing homework, playing an instrument, creating an artwork, playing outside, playing inside, helping out. These home-based activities are as important as the things your children learn at school in terms of building knowledge, developing skills and creating a sense of one's place in the world.

These days there are numerous opportunities for children to be 'on screen'. They can watch TV and DVDs, surf the net, and play interactive games on consoles and mobile phones. For many children, watching TV or surfing the Internet is their default leisure activity – the thing they always do when there is free time.

So how much screen time is acceptable? Experts seem to agree that two hours a day is about right for children over five, one hour for children two to five, and no screen time for those under two. For many parents this will mean working with children to wean them off excessive screen time. For others it will be about putting things in place to help kids avoid the lure of the screen further down the track.

Here are some suggestions that may help:

- If your child is using screens more than two hours a day, work with them to gradually decrease their screen time by about fifteen minutes a day until you reach the two-hour mark.
- Work with older children to get the daily balance right between TV, DVDs, the Internet and games.
- Sit down with your children at the beginning of the week and go through the TV guide together; try to pick shows that are educational as well as fun and shows that appear on commercial-free channels.
- Consider having screen-free days two to three days each week.
- Avoid having family meals in front of the TV (see page 135).
- Think carefully about the number of screens you want in your house – the more screens the greater the likelihood they will be used.
- Don't put TVs in bedrooms.

If your teenager wants to have a computer in their bedroom for study purposes negotiate its use, making a clear delineation between study and leisure time. Just as importantly, make sure you positively reinforce alternative behaviours to screen time such as reading, socialising with family and friends and doing arts and crafts.

92. Encourage formal exercise

By formal exercise I mean any form of movement that you (and your child) enjoy and feel comfortable doing.

The Raising Children Network's website, raisingchildren.net.au, has some very useful and practical advice about how to encourage your child to exercise sensibly and safely. These tips are not very different from what we, as adults, should be doing anyway; if we're trying to encourage our children to maintain healthy activity levels we'll also be looking after ourselves and our own health (a real win–win if ever there was one).

Many kids love to be outdoors and be active, but if your child needs a little more encouragement suggest they try a range of sports and activities – if your child enjoys an activity and is good at it they will be more likely to persist.

Up until the age of around seven most children enjoy unstructured activities such as playing in playgrounds and just running around. After this many children will be ready for more structured sports and games that involve rules.

In addition to the physical benefits, children involved in structured sports and games also learn key life skills such as interacting with others, the consequences of obeying (or not obeying) rules, and how to cope with winning and losing.

93. Encourage informal exercise and incidental activity

Ultimately it doesn't really matter what activities your child is involved in, as long as they're moving for at least a few hours every day.

Exercise doesn't have to be organised sport; it might just be informal running around or playing in a playground or helping out with household chores such as washing the car or sweeping up leaves.

As well as informal exercise, incidental activity can make up part of your (and your child's) day. Try the following:

- Walk to school and the local shops rather than drive.
- Walk up the stairs rather than take the elevator or escalator.
- Go for a walk (or what my kids like to call 'an adventure') rather than watch TV or play computer games.

If you really want your child to enjoy exercise and activity make it fun and give them lots of positive feedback. These two simple strategies apply to pretty much everything in this book – and they work!

94. Select physical activities that reflect your child's interests (not yours)

Nowhere is the phenomenon of the over-involved parent more obvious than on the sports field. While many parents have a realistic approach to their child's abilities, some parents insist on reliving past sporting glories (or making up for sporting failures) through their kids. Go to a netball court or soccer field on a Saturday morning and you will see at least a couple of parents urging their child towards a level of achievement that may be impossible for that child at that time. I remember hearing a radio announcer talking about the experience of organising his son's hockey team. The other fathers were so anxious about their respective sons' achievements that the radio announcer suggested they form a fathers' team as a means of distraction. It worked by leaving the boys free to get on with their game.

The message here is this: select sports or games that suit your child and will help them develop skills. Take into account your child's personality, interests and capabilities. Are they competitive? Are they a team player or do they prefer activities they can concentrate on alone? Do they have good hand–eye coordination? Are they big and strong or fast and nimble? By doing this you will ensure your child gets pleasure out of the activity and be inspired to continue on into adult life.

Isobel, aged twelve, has a great deal of natural physical talent. Although small for her age, she is strong, extremely flexible, fast and virtually fearless. Her parents have encouraged her to try a variety of sports, but from the age of eight, gymnastics was her main pursuit, an activity that allowed Isobel's strengths to really come to the fore. But just as teachers started putting her into competitions and talking 'Olympic potential', Isobel decided to quit. Her parents were worried that Isobel was squandering her talent, but then decided to sit back a bit and wait for another interest to emerge. In the last year, Isobel has taken up surfing and contemporary dance, and is good at both. Isobel loves physical activity but has worked out that she doesn't like lots of rules and regulations. While doing gymnastics she often complained about this aspect of the sport. Now with surfing she sets her own challenges, and with dancing she gets to combine the pure pleasure of physical activity with her strong creative instincts.

95. Establish healthy sleep routines

Sleep is vitally beneficial for the health and happiness of our growing children. Sleep allows their bodies and minds to recuperate, recover and regenerate. Sleep allows their rapidly growing brains to process information from the day and file what's relevant and important.

The whole sleep issue is one of the more perplexing aspects of parenting. Just as you think you have it worked out, the patterns change. New parents are convinced their babies sleep far less than other peoples' babies and live in hope that their baby or toddler will sleep past 5 am, just once. By contrast, parents of adolescents seem to invest an inordinate amount of time and energy in trying to get their kids out of bed in time for school.

Despite these sorts of age-specific fluctuations there are some principles in terms of establishing good sleep routines that, as a parent, you should be able to apply at any time during childhood, from about three years old and upwards.

First of all, how much sleep do kids need? This varies quite a lot according to the individual, just as it does for adults, but as a guideline aim for:

- ten to thirteen hours of sleep for three to five year olds
- ten to eleven hours of sleep for six to nine year olds
- nine to ten hours of sleep for ten year olds and above.

Keep track of how much your child sleeps to make sure your expectations are reasonable. You may have to make some adjustments, depending on your child and your lifestyle. An eight-year-old child who is being put to bed at 7.30 pm then wakes up with the birds at 5 am may need a later bedtime. Once you have determined an appropriate number of hours of sleep, try the following suggestions for establishing a routine:

- Establish a bedtime and a lights-off time. Many children aged eight and up benefit from a quiet half hour with a book before the lights are turned off.
- Establish pre-bed routines. This may involve getting out clothes for the morning and packing away homework and toys. It will certainly involve brushing teeth and going to the toilet.
- Younger children up to the age of ten will enjoy a story before bed. This allows them to settle down for the night, and creates some time for end-of-the-day bonding between parent and child.
- Be clear and firm about saying goodnight. Let your child know that once you have said goodnight, and switched off the lights, you expect them to stay in bed.
- Try to encourage your children to wake at approximately the same time each day, even on weekends.

There are some common mistakes parents make that prevent their children having a deep and restful sleep. Work with your child to avoid the following:

- sweet food and drinks before bed (particularly caffeinated soft drinks and sports drinks)
- a late dinner (try to eat at least two hours before your kids' bedtime)
- overstimulating TV shows or computer games
- falling asleep in front of the TV
- doing homework just before bed (encourage your child to stop at least half an hour before bedtime – definitely no homework in bed).

Make sleep a priority for your children, and watch things improve! If you don't prioritise sleep, they'll always find other 'more important' things to do. Good sleep practices, established early, will be of benefit throughout childhood and particularly during adolescence when the demands on your child's time (the reasons not to sleep) increase dramatically.

96. Teach your child how to relax

Some parents may think it's odd talking about children and relaxation. Children don't have the weight of the world on their shoulders like adults do. They don't have to work and earn money and deal with office politics and figure out how to pay the mortgage. They get to play, have fun, and when school gets a bit too much there is always another fortnight of school holidays around the corner.

Because of this, parents are prone to brush aside their children's worries, viewing them as minor. A child who is fretting about her homework may be told, 'Don't worry, it's easy.' Or a child who is upset about a friendship might hear from his parent, 'It's silly to care what someone else thinks.'

The reality is that children do worry and it does help to equip them with coping mechanisms that will serve them now and into the future.

Anxiety has psychological causes, but its manifestations are physical. Doctors and psychologists have come to recognise that they can help patients calm the mind by calming the body. This physical calming gives people the space they need to step back from a problem and make a better assessment of it, rather than simply reacting to the panic that is causing their heart to race and their breathing to shorten. This calming works for children in exactly the same way it works for adults.

There are many approaches to relaxation, none of which is necessarily better or worse. One method you could try with your child is usually referred to as 'visual imagery relaxation'. It is most effective in creating feelings of calmness and tranquillity. It can be practised anywhere but is typically easiest to do in a quiet, peaceful location. It's a form of relaxation that many children love because it allows for the use of imagination and creativity. Start by following the instructions below, but feel free to experiment and come up with your own ideas:

- Help make your child comfortable and ask them to focus on breathing slowly (it might help to instruct them lie down and close their eyes).
- Ask them to imagine themselves in a beautiful location where everything is ideal. They could be in a lovely holiday spot or in Grandpa's garden or Grandma's kitchen making cookies. They could be walking in a beautiful forest or on a favourite beach. Or they might just be in front of the fire at home on a rainy Sunday afternoon.
- Talk about how calm and relaxing everything is. Don't describe the scene to your child, but ask them to think about particular details: ask them to imagine the colour of the water, the smell of the cookies, the feel of sand, the crunch of leaves underfoot.
- Encourage them to involve all of their senses and assure them they can return to this special place whenever they need to.

Meditation can help your child live in the moment. Meditation is not, despite the many misconceptions out there, a skill that helps people 'switch off'; in contrast, those who meditate feel more 'switched on'. It's not about sleeping or resting or 'zoning out', but rather it's about being fully awake and engaged in life.

Older children, particularly, can be taught a fast and easy form of mediation that will assist them in all aspects of their lives, whether it's coping with exams, dealing with difficult social problems, or as an aid to overcoming the frustrations involved in learning a new and challenging skill in areas such as sport and music.

Try the following so you can then teach your child:

- Find a comfortable sitting position, either cross-legged on the floor or in a chair.
- Close your eyes.
- Start to focus on your breathing. Think 'in' when you breathe in, and 'out' when you breathe out.
- Repeat this over and over again, focusing on these two simple words.
- If you get distracted, gently ease your mind back to your breath and to your repetition of 'in' and 'out'.

Encourage your child to practise a few times a day, even if only for a few minutes. They will gradually master the skill and know how to apply it instantly in difficult or stressful situations.

97. Make time for doing nothing

Obviously we need to be 'on' during certain activities, but how many of us allow ourselves or our children the opportunity to switch off and take a break?

A complaint you'll often hear these days from grandparents and older teachers is that parents are not letting their children get bored. What the older generation knows – the generation that grew up without all the technological gadgetry that defines modern-day life – is the art of doing nothing can often lead to some wonderfully creative moments. Children who are inside on a rainy day and not allowed to watch TV will do things like make cubby houses, put on plays, invent imaginary friends, write stories, build houses out of cards and rearrange the family photos or the cans of food at the bottom of the pantry. The art of doing nothing is an important one to develop. Dealing with nothing time, and even bore- dom, can assist in the development of creativity, innovation, imagination, reflection, introspection and interaction with others.

The other reason why it's important to encourage down time in otherwise busy days is that it creates the opportunity for a little bit of mental and physical rest, particularly after the age of, say, three, when many children give up their afternoon rest.

In a fascinating project from the book *The Power of Full Engagement* by Jim Loehr and Tony Schwartz, researchers studied the top ten ten- nis players to see what separated them from the lower-ranked players. After measuring a number of physical, physiological and psychological variables, the researchers discovered that the best players were signifi- cantly different from the others in one important area: their resting pulse rate between points, which was significantly lower in the top ten compared with the other players.

What does this mean? These top players were much better and more efficient at resting and conserving valuable energy and resources when they didn't need to be playing – in other words, they were better at switching off when they didn't need to be switched on.

I believe this skill is a valuable one for our kids to learn in all kinds of situations. How much energy do we waste when we're 'on' all the time? How much energy could we save if we learned how to rest more often and more effectively?

With this in mind, I encourage you, as parents, to teach and encourage your child to 'actively rest'; to plan for and utilise the benefits of short, regular breaks. Help your child pace themselves through a day, a week and even a year rather than going 'like a bull at a gate', which often leads to some sort of crash (you know what I mean, that end-of-school-term mood when anything and everything can lead to tears and tantrums).

Nine-year-old Alex is a keen soccer player. He used to get up at the crack of dawn every Saturday morning to get ready for that day's game. He'd practise in the backyard, talk at a hundred miles an hour about his team, the rival team and the game plan, and play soccer games on the computer. Once he'd get to the ground he'd tear around with his team mates, waiting for the game to start. The first half of his game was generally excellent, but by the second half he was exhausted. He'd lose concentration and focus; more often than not he'd get a stitch and have to come off the field. After talking to the coach, his parents decided to institute a new regime. Alex now spends quiet time with a book for at least half an hour on Saturday mornings. His dad does another half an hour of drills with him in the backyard, then nothing more until he gets to the ground. Before the game, the coach gets all the boys to do some stretches in a steady, focused way. Not only is Alex playing a better game, but he has learnt an important lesson about how to pace himself that he can apply to other parts of his life.

98. Encourage your child to develop problem-solving strategies

We can't stop our children from experiencing pain, nor can we eliminate problems from their lives. Facing up to and dealing with life's adversities are the things that help us grow as human beings. Problems are the lessons we need to experience in order to become functioning adults. One of best things you can do as a parent is teach your child how to take an active approach to reducing worry and solving problems, rather than avoiding them.

Next time your child comes to you with a problem try this approach:

- Help define the problem. What's going on? Encourage your child to answer the question as specifically and as clearly as possible. Help them break down big problems into smaller ones.
- Brainstorm potential solutions to the problem. Generate as many solutions as you can without evaluating them; rather, encourage your child to let their imagination run wild.
- Talk about the list of potential solutions. Examine the advantages and disadvantages of each possible solution. Give a positive score to good solutions and a minus score to the ones that aren't so good.
- Help your child choose the solution they think will work best for them and their situation, but don't be afraid to remind them of all the potential advantages and disadvantages; highlight long-term consequences rather than just immediate ones.
- Help generate an action plan. Ask your child what they think they will need to do to make this plan work. Get them to be as specific as possible.

- Encourage your child to put their plan into action. Tell them that if they do nothing they will achieve nothing. At least by trying they have a chance of achieving something.
- Together, evaluate the outcome. Did it work? If not, can they modify the plan?

99. Identify significant mental health problems (and know when to get help)

This book is about promoting happiness and resilience in children, and I'm confident it will help you address most of the issues commonly faced by parents. However, the unfortunate reality is that some children will experience psychological issues beyond the 'normal'. A small but significant proportion, for example, will experience the more common forms of psychological disorders including depression and anxiety. Others might develop significant problems with their weight or suffer from learning difficulties.

How do you know when normal becomes abnormal? Most parents know when something's not right, but, in simple terms, be aware:

- if a problem persists longer than you'd expect it to
- if an issue is significantly impacting your child's daily functioning – their mood, sleep, appetite, energy levels, attendance at school or social activities, their interpersonal relationships or their academic performance
- if other people around your child are concerned.

In most instances I'd recommend doing what you can on your own first. This might include slowing down the pace of family life a little, taking a holiday, making a point of spending one-on-one time with your child. It could also include having a chat to other family members and friends about some of the issues that may be affecting your child. If the problem persists, if you're feeling out of your depth or if you don't think you have the resources to manage whatever is going on then it's probably better to seek expert assistance sooner rather than later. A good first point of contact is always your child's school and the school counselling service. Next step is the family doctor, who will provide advice and, if necessary, referrals to other health professionals. There is a list of Recommended Resources on page 164 that may be of use.

Of course there will be times when it feels like you're losing touch with your child. Try not to jump the gun. Encourage them to open up but be aware of pushing them too hard or expecting too much too soon. Let them know you are there for them when they're ready (and really be there!).

100. Love your child for who they are

All children should be loved for who and what they are, as opposed to who and what we'd like them to be. Loving them doesn't mean trying to change their underlying personality, character or their core strengths; instead it's about working with their strengths to help them develop.

Your love and support are vital to your child's development. Their personality and strengths will be different from yours – they'll surprise you, they'll annoy you, they'll make you proud – and it's these differences that will provide some of the best (and worst!) moments in your life. When it comes down to it, children teach us acceptance, patience, understanding ... the list goes on. The bond you have will be one of the closest you will ever experience, so cherish it, warts and all.

Together, aim to:

- be tolerant
- nurture relationships
- give and forgive
- face adversity
- avoid assumptions
- respect differences
- use compassion and humour
- listen
- celebrate life.

Recommended resources

Books:

Alexander, Stephanie, *Kitchen Garden Cooking for Kids*, Lantern, Melbourne, 2003 .

Covey, Stephen R, *7 Habits of Highly Effective People: Resorting the Character Ethic*, Simon & Schuster, New York, 1989.

CSIRO, *The CSIRO Wellbeing Plan for Kids*, Penguin Books, Melbourne, 2009.

Kirk, David, *Little Miss Spider at Sunny Patch School*, Scholastic Press, New York, 2000.

Loehr, Jim and Schwartz, Tony, *The Power of Full Engagement*, Allen & Unwin, Sydney, 2003.

Parry Heide, Florence and Van Clief, Sylvia, *That's What Friends Are For*, Candlewick Press, New York, 2003.

Reynolds, Peter H, *Ish*, Candlewick Press, New York, 2004.

Seligman, Martin, *The Optimistic Child*, Random House, Sydney, 1995.

Sendak, Maurice, *Where the Wild Things Are*, Harper & Row, New York, 1963.

Sharp, Timothy, *100 Ways to Happiness: a guide for busy people*, Penguin Books, Melbourne, 2008.

Sharp, Timothy, *The Good Sleep Guide: 10 steps to better sleep and how to break the worry cycle*, Penguin Books, Melbourne, 2001 (available in e-book form at thehappinessinstitute.com).

Movies:

Benigni, Roberto, *Life is Beautiful (La Vita é Bella)*, Miramax Films, 1997.

Anderson, Stephen J, *Meet the Robinsons*, Buena Vista Entertainment, 2007.

Websites:

authentichappiness.sas.upenn.edu

beyondblue.org.au

makingchanges.com.au

moodmanager.com.au

raisingchildren.net.au

thehappinessinstitute.com

www.psychology.org.au/ReferralService/About

Acknowledgements

Firstly, thank you to my loving family. Tali and Coby, I hope the many hours that have been required to write this book have in no way detracted from my efforts to raise you as happy children!

Secondly, this book also owes thanks to my parents. Despite experiencing many of the challenges and setbacks so many parents face, my mother and father never left me and my two siblings with any doubt that they loved us and thought we were special. We always knew they would be there to support us when we needed help.

Thirdly, I'm so grateful to the team at Penguin, especially to Ingrid Ohlsson and Julie Gibbs for having faith in this book, and to Bethan Waterhouse, Angela Wade, Claire de Medici, Brooke Clarke and Catherine Page for so expertly helping me shape it into what you now have before you. Thanks also to Danie Pout and Evi Oetomo for their wonderful design.

And finally, an enormous thanks to all the members of The Happiness Institute community. Through your attendance of our seminars, courses and coaching, via your emails and suggestions, and as a result of your contributions to my web blog, many have directly and indirectly, knowingly and unknowingly, assisted with the development of my ideas and with the formulation of this book – for that, again, I'm grateful.

Index